ENDORSEMENTS

Dr. Andy Young has a way of taking the extremely challenging role of psychological counseling in crisis situations and applying a practical, caring method of counseling that can help others cope with their chaos. This book is thought-provoking, illustrated with true stories, and is a great read for psychologists, emergency first responders, pastors, health care professionals and social workers—anyone who cares for those in crisis circumstances. Dr. Young's greatest attribute is his gift of serving those most in need.

Roger Ellis, Chief of Police (Retired)
Lubbock Police Department
Lubbock, Texas

I have had the opportunity to work with Dr. Young both professionally and personally. Dr. Young's book gives the reader insight into critical incidents that are often unseen. Furthermore, this insight is that of a mental health professional. Dr. Young has the ability to give authentic behavior assessments on scene that, in turn, help incident commanders make crucial decisions. In this book, you will read of some decisions that went well and of others that produced learning points for all involved. This book will take you through a range of emotions and keep you reading until the finish.

Brandon Pierpoint, President
Texas Association of Hostage Negotiations

I have co-authored one of the leading books in the field of crisis negotiation, and that book is used internationally to train negotiators. Although it talks about emotions, the crisis response, stress, PTSD, etc., it does so in a technical and clinical manner; in a way that can be used to teach. Dr. Young's book covers those same topics at a personal level that conveys to the reader the depth and difficulty of dealing with those emotions. His book speaks to the heart of the reader. That is something sorely needed and has been lacking in the field until now. In the future, I would require officers in my introductory negotiation classes to read his book.

At its very heart, Dr. Young's book deals with the emotions expressed when people are in crisis. And at that, he does an outstanding job. His is a book about emotions and how those emotions influence negotiators and the negotiation process. Seldom has anyone ever done it as succinctly, clearly, concisely, and as expertly as Dr. Young has done. While his book is not a primer on negotiations or the negotiation process, it should be mandatory reading for every negotiator, every tactical officer, every commander, and every patrol officer. Dr. Young does what no other book has attempted: he explores the human drama inherent within the crisis incident that all responders must ultimately address and deal with. Further, he does it in a way that enables the reader to fully understand the range of emotions often encountered in these incidents.

Although many officers would like to believe it so, the reality is that law enforcement does not work in an emotional and psychological vacuum. The cases presented by Dr. Young can go a long way in eliminating those beliefs and perceptions and lead all of us to a fuller understanding of the human drama we must deal with on a daily basis to be successful in this career.

Wayman Mullins, Author
Crisis Negotiations: Managing Critical Incidents and Hostage Situations in Law Enforcement and Corrections

FIGHT OR FLIGHT

NEGOTIATING CRISIS ON THE FRONT LINE

FIGHT OR FLIGHT

NEGOTIATING CRISIS ON THE FRONT LINE

DR. ANDREW T. YOUNG, *LPC-S, NCC*

eGenCo

Copyright © 2016 – by Dr. Andrew T. Young

Published by eGenCo

All rights reserved. This book is protected by the copyright laws of the United States of America. This book may not be copied or reprinted for commercial gain or profit. The use of short quotations or occasional page copying for personal or group study is permitted and encouraged. Permission for other usages must be obtained from eGenCo or the author. Scripture quotations marked (NIV) are taken from the Holy Bible, New International Version®, NIV®. Copyright © 1973, 1978, 1984, 2011 by Biblica, Inc.™ Used by permission of Zondervan. All rights reserved worldwide. www.zondervan.com The "NIV" and "New International Version" are trademarks registered in the United States Patent and Trademark Office by Biblica, Inc.™ Scripture quotations marked (NIrV) are taken from the Holy Bible, New International Reader's Version®, NIrV® Copyright © 1995, 1996, 1998 by Biblica, Inc.™ Used by permission of Zondervan. All rights reserved worldwide. www.zondervan.com The "NIrV" and "New International Reader's Version" are trademarks registered in the United States Patent and Trademark Office by Biblica, Inc.™ "Scripture quotations taken from the New American Standard Bible®, Copyright © 1960, 1962, 1963, 1968, 1971, 1972, 1973, 1975, 1977, 1995 by The Lockman Foundation Used by permission." (www.Lockman.org) American Standard Version (ASV) is recognized in most of the world, as well as the Unites States, as public domain.

eGenCo

Generation Culture Transformation
Specializing in publishing for generation culture change

eGenCo
824 Tallow Hill Road
Chambersburg, PA 17202, USA
Phone: 717-461-3436
Email: info@egen.co
Website: www.egen.co

 facebook.com/egenbooks

 youtube.com/egenpub

 egen.co/blog

 pinterest.com/eGenDMP

 twitter.com/eGenDMP

 instagram.com/egenco_dmp

Publisher's Cataloging-in-Publication Data
Young, Andrew
Fight or Flight. Negotiating Crisis on the Front Line.;
by Dr. Andrew T. Young.
244 pages cm.
ISBN: 978-1-68019-963-5 paperback
        978-1-68019-964-2 ebook
        978-1-68019-965-9 ebook
1. Crisis management. 2. Law enforcement. 3. Trauma. I. Title
2015954237

Cover design and page layout by Kevin Lepp, www.kmlstudio.com

This book is dedicated to the men and women
in emergency services who are called upon
all too often to do an impossible job.

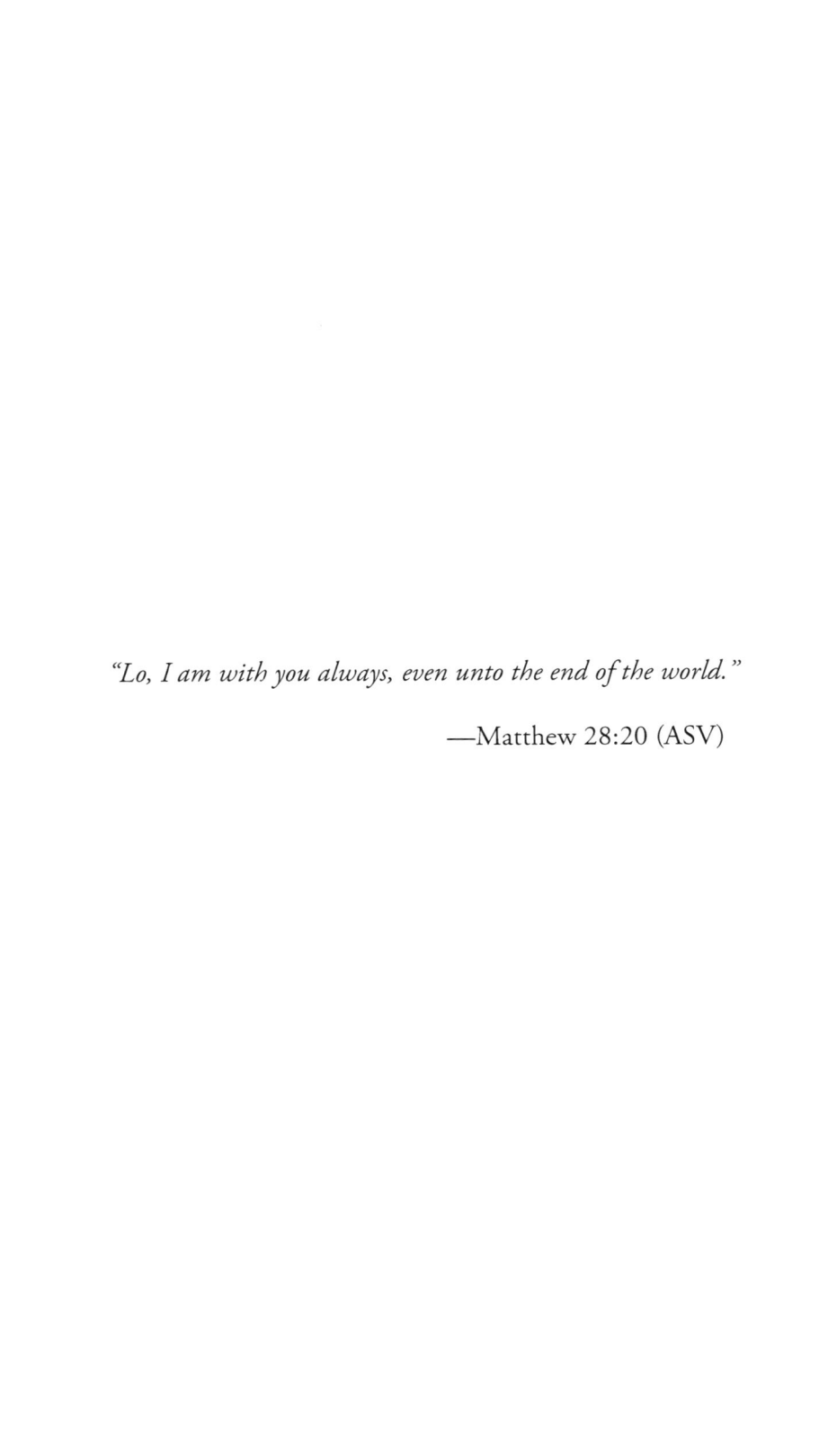

"Lo, I am with you always, even unto the end of the world."

—Matthew 28:20 (ASV)

TABLE OF CONTENTS

	Introduction	xxi
Chapter One	The Job that Found Me	1
Chapter Two	Officer Down	9
Chapter Three	The Negotiation	21
Chapter Four	Rising to the Challenge	47
Chapter Five	Nothing Left to Live For	59
Chapter Six	The Bearer of Bad News	81
Chapter Seven	"This Can't Be True"	93
Chapter Eight	Bringing Order to the Chaos	121
Chapter Nine	Violence in the Home	135
Chapter Ten	Street Cred	151
Chapter Eleven	When a Cop Has to Kill	159
Chapter Twelve	Helping the Good Guys Cope	181
Chapter Thirteen	Why Am I Still Doing This?	193
	References and Resources	205
	Abbreviations	207
	Glossary	209
	About the Author	217

FOREWORD

The year was 1995, and it was my first time speaking with an individual who was standing over the pedestrian rail on the Golden Gate Bridge (GGB) in San Francisco, CA, contemplating suicide. I was a member of the California Highway Patrol (CHP) for over 23 years, with the majority of that time spent working around the GGB. The bridge was part of the jurisdiction of Marin County where I was stationed. Prior to working on the bridge, I had no idea the number of suicide/mental health incidents that took place there. I discovered there are generally 35-60 confirmed cases of suicide from that bridge each year and an unknown number of unconfirmed cases (e.g., jumping at night or in the fog). Also, that number or more individuals are detained by the CHP and taken to local hospitals for mental health evaluations.

So, back to my first contact with a suicidal person on the bridge: I received a radio call to respond to a person in danger on the bridge and arrived at the scene just a few minutes later. As I drove to the site, I wondered the entire time what the hell I would say to this person. You see, I had no training for cases like this—people who are seemingly on the verge of suicide. I thought to myself, 'If I say the wrong thing, this person may jump'. I literally had no idea how to handle a situation like this. This sort of event was not taught in the academy.

When I got to the location, I saw a young lady in her mid-thirties, decently dressed and groomed. She was standing on a piece of the bridge we called the "chord," a metal I-beam paralleling the bridge. She had traversed the four-foot pedestrian rail and now stood quietly and solemnly, probably contemplating what might be her last few moments on earth. I slowly approached her, introduced myself, and asked some general questions. She was crying and looked like she was in a lot of emotional pain. I remember hoping that I looked calm on the outside––I was shaking on the inside and stumbling through every sentence I spoke. All I really had going for me at that moment was empathy. I did not want to see this young lady lose her life, but I couldn't come up with anything to say that I thought was going to help her. If I couldn't make sense of the situation myself—how in the world was I going to help her? It was amazing to me during my time with her that she worked *with* me to keep a conversation going for about 30 minutes, at which point she made the decision to come back over the rail and get some professional help. I truly think she really did want to live, but also probably had pity for me, thinking something like, 'This poor officer has no idea what he's doing.'

Looking back on this incident after my many years of experience, I said about every wrong thing a trained negotiator would never say to her. Things like, "I understand," "Things will get better," and "It can't be that bad."

It was after several calls like this one that I realized that any individual helping a person in crisis had to work quickly to establish a genuine connection. Some of the very first steps I learned that worked well for me include: approaching the subject with a calm demeanor; saying "hello," along with my name; asking general questions to start a path of connectivity that can move along a conversation – not an interrogation; displaying genuine interest in the individual and the things they want to discuss; moving the conversation to future activities (hope); conveying empathy; and establishing continued contact at eye level with the person.

That day on the Bridge I spent talking with that young lady changed me forever. I loved working on the Bridge. It's a beautiful area where you meet people from all over the world. But the Bridge also has a dark side – it sometimes is the last visit to a beautiful, powerful, and majestic place, where people plan to, and do, take their own life.

My point is this: I had no official or even transitory training on how to handle people with mental or behavioral issues who were experiencing suicidal ideation or in the throes of taking their own life. I wish I had this book available prior to even graduating from the academy in 1990. You see, this book by my friend, Dr. Young, is not just a recollection of his past experiences showing extreme cases that law enforcement officers deal with. This book delves into the minds and thought processes of those on the front lines and the individuals who come into contact with them. Dr. Young perfectly portrays what it's like to negotiate with folks bent on doing evil, those suffering from a mental illness or years of abuse, to name a few. Through his eyes, you'll be on scene with negotiators and SWAT teams, feeling what goes through their minds and lives each day they wear that uniform.

The way a trained negotiator handles a suicidal subject, bank robber, or barricaded individual is an art to watch. For example, a negotiator will engage a subject who may be highly emotional and threatening hostages and move the individual to a point where the person willingly surrenders—and even thanks the negotiator for their honesty and empathy. It is truly amazing to watch a seasoned negotiator at work. Now couple that with a trained mental health professional like Dr. Young who goes above and beyond to access law enforcement's crisis training, and you have, in my opinion, the best-case scenario for a positive outcome, no matter the event. More and more, police departments are now relying on the skills and knowledge of trained mental health professionals to assist them with everything from domestic disputes to officer line-of-duty deaths to working with individuals who are experiencing a mental health break.

From disturbing domestic calls to suicidal individuals to officers killed in the line of duty, Dr. Young has seen and experienced it all. He relays his real-life experiences in a way which allows a behind-the-scenes look at what is really happening inside the thoughts and minds of officers and their families when a line-of-duty death occurs, what officers feel and go through when they take the life of another person to protect the public and themselves, and the important role mental health professionals now play in law enforcement.

I met Dr. Young at a National Hostage Negotiation Conference in 2013, where we both spoke. He has gained national respect for his ability to connect with people, his empathy towards his fellow man, and his work assisting officers and their families in dealing with a myriad of crises that come with doing this type of work.

Like I stated earlier, I wish I had this book prior to pinning on my badge. Whether you are an officer, chief of police, sheriff, negotiator, or citizen wishing to understand what it's like to be "on the job," I am positive you'll find this book educational, entertaining, filled with insight, and thought-provoking. Most importantly, it may help you save a life.

Kevin R. Briggs
Sergeant, California Highway Patrol (Ret.)
Author of *Guardian of the Golden Gate*
Marin County, CA

PREFACE

Sometime during the year 2010, I decided to go back through ten years of records and tally all the emergency calls I had responded to as a counselor and member of the Victim Services Crisis Team at the Lubbock Police Department. I stopped counting at 500. Since that time in 2010, I've been involved with many, many more. The stories told herein are but a *small* and *exceptional* sample of these many calls.

This short book cannot do justice to the myriad of domestic disputes or the frequent "natural death" callouts that occur when most people are asleep and have no idea that someone nearby has been suddenly stricken with a personal tragedy, like the night I sat alone with a woman in her 70's who had no one else to console her after her husband had passed away. Then there was the young man who had called the police saying he was thinking about killing himself, though he really just needed someone to talk to during a lonely holiday. On another occasion, I showed up at a residence to help establish some peace between a couple and their "depressed and rebellious" teenage son. When their argument, earlier that night, had escalated into a family fight, they didn't know what else to do except dial 911.

Unlike the examples mentioned above, the incidents I have chosen to address in this book, for the most part, include a spectrum of horrific crises and some criminal activity. Most of the time, I will not use real names when speaking of a victim(s) or perpetrator. However, I will often use the term "bad guy" when referring to a person who, without a doubt, has committed a crime. (My cop friends use more colorful language—"scum bag" comes to mind.)

I proudly serve and assist the officers of the Lubbock Police Department, who do the best they can with the available information and resources. I've experienced up-close and firsthand the immense pressure of their responsibilities. Thus, I can say with certainty, that law enforcement officers and emergency services personnel do some of the most difficult and thankless work, nonstop, every day and every night, amidst various circumstances of chaos and crisis—many times finding themselves in dangerous predicaments where the only thing that's sure is relying on their wits, training, and the guy backing them.

In addition to relaying some information that I've learned along the way about how to handle chaotic and stressful situations, I'll reflect on some advice that I've given as a negotiator and counselor. I'll also take a look at some critical decisions that our police officers have had to make, which resulted in a positive ending. However, I'll discuss just as many cases that resulted in a not-so-positive ending. I will share what I've learned in the hope that this honesty and vulnerability will help other individuals (both professional and nonprofessional) as they encounter similar emergencies and disastrous situations.

My purpose in writing this book is to help others, who may also be in this line of work, by sharing my stories, experiences, teachable moments and lessons learned. I hope that sharing these things might educate those who only had a vague understanding of what happens on the other side of the yellow tape and in amongst the flashing red and blue lights. I am an educator at heart, so I trust that what I am about to share will be beneficial. These are my stories.

ACKNOWLEDGMENTS

Thanks to my wife, Stacy. While I am out with the police, she entrusts my safety to God, takes care of the many responsibilities at home, and supports me fully, even when this work adversely affects me, personally.

Thanks to all the men and women of the Lubbock Police Department who have been notably supportive of me and the Crisis Team, and who have, over the years, entrusted me with a serious responsibility.

Thanks to everyone who has served or continues to serve on the Victim Services Crisis Team at the Lubbock Police Department. It has been a privilege to work alongside such an outstanding group of people.

Thanks to the SWAT and Negotiating Teams at the Lubbock Police Department. I have always considered it an amazing honor to be a part of these teams and this work.

Thanks to Brian Lankford for taking me on the first EMS ride-along and infecting me with a passion for emergency services.

Thanks to Seydia Adkins who saw this Acknowledgments page first.

Thanks to Kevin Briggs who encouraged me to pull the pin and pursue writing this book.

Thanks to Doug Allen who connected me with Vishal Jetnarayan and all the lovely people at eGenCo Publishing. And thank you, Doug, for helping me navigate some of the difficult theological waters associated with crises.

Thanks to my parents and grandparents who helped lay the foundation in me that's led to my being able to bring a level head and calm demeanor to a crisis situation. They also instilled integrity and frankness within me, which has proven invaluable in this vocation.

Thanks to Rebekah Helman with whom it has been such a pleasure to work and write.

INTRODUCTION

Officer Rodney R. Kendricks
July 26, 1967 – July 8, 2001

Sergeant Kevin Cox
June 30, 1963 – July 13, 2001

The Police Department of Lubbock, Texas had not lost an officer in the line of duty for ten years. That changed in July of 2001, when a sergeant was killed just two days after one of our motorcycle officers had been laid to rest.

I had never attended a funeral or any type of memorial service for a law enforcement officer. What's more, I had recently been advised that in my capacity, attending such a service wasn't the best idea. I went anyway. It seemed like the right thing to do.

Exactly one year earlier, I had embarked on a new endeavor as a volunteer crisis counselor with the police department in addition to teaching Psychology, Counseling, and other courses in the Behavioral Sciences Department at Lubbock Christian University. I was also working on my doctoral degree at Texas Tech.

Each month, on a Friday or Saturday night from 7:00 p.m. to 2:00 a.m., and every once in a while during the week, I would respond to a variety of emergency calls, assisting the police whenever they needed a mental health professional (MHP) to help with any victims. Meanwhile, I completed a certification in Critical Incident Stress Management (CISM), and a group of us, both officers as well as mental health professionals, were in the process of hammering out our policies and procedures manual that would help establish our CISM program. The purpose of this program would be to help our own departmental personnel if ever needed.

Suddenly our officers were trying to cope with the loss of two of their own. Consequently, the CISM team was asked to do what we could to help, whether we were ready or not. As I attempted to provide support to all those trying to deal with one officer's death and then another, I remembered the advice that I should not go to either funeral. Common sense dictated that I, as a counselor, should not become personally overwhelmed with any part of the incident, including a ceremony where many people would be expressing their sorrow as they remembered and honored the fallen.

Although I agreed that it wouldn't be wise to risk getting bogged down in my own grief, I decided that I should attend both funerals, for various reasons.

First and foremost, these two men had given their lives, and although I only knew one of them in passing, I thought it important that I respectfully pay my regards. Second, I wanted to be there in order to provide any assistance needed, especially to some of the officers with whom I made acquaintance. Finally, if I did feel overwhelmed by the service, I knew I could turn to my wife for support or to any one of a number of professional counselors or friends. But honestly, I didn't think that attending such a service would bother me too much. At this point in my life I simply thought that in addition to my education, I had acquired enough training and personal preparation in emergency services to handle an emotional atmosphere.

An example from my personal life might be helpful. From an early age I'd been acquainted with death a few times, including the time my grandmother moved into my room when I was in high school as she

Introduction

and my grandfather sought care for her cancer. We watched her slowly die for about six months. The night she died, I remember the mortuary service coming to pick up her body. We all stood there outside my room as they carried her out in a black body bag. I even remember one of the mortuary service attendants commenting on how light she was.

Another example of the personal preparation began in 1998, while teaching a General Psychology class at Lubbock Christian University. There I met Brian Lankford, a student and a paramedic. In one of his essays for my class, Brian wrote about his experiences in emergency services, which happened to pique my interest. After the final exam, as Brian left class, I asked him if I could ride along in the ambulance sometime.

"Sure," he nodded, "Here's my pager number. Give me a call whenever you're ready."

Not long after that conversation, I was able to join Brian on one of his 24-hour shifts. I specifically remember the first call that evening, helping pick up an elderly man after he had fallen and become stuck between the toilet and the wall—quite a low-grade, introductory exposure to crisis.

Not only did I have the opportunity to ride with an ambulance team on several occasions, but when Brian later accepted a position with AeroCare, an air ambulance service, I also got the chance to take a few exciting helicopter rides. My last air trip with Brian occurred not long before I joined the police department's Victim Services Crisis Team. A man had shot himself in the head in the middle of the night. AeroCare was informed that the victim needed to be transported to University Medical Center, the level-one trauma center in Lubbock. And so, off we went.

A night landing fascinated me, and during this flight I sat riveted as the pilot maneuvered the aircraft around wires and poles, a tree here, a house there, and all the while, keeping an eye out for other vehicles, people, animals, and any other objects, stationary or moving, with just a spotlight.

Once we landed, I remained in the helicopter while Brian and the flight nurse attended to the injured man and loaded him into the chopper. As we rose up in the air, Brian began to do chest compressions. After a time, Brian, who was also a paramedic trainer and knowing that I was CPR certified, said, "Andy, why don't you take over." I put on some gloves and assumed his place while he pointed out the gunshot wound in the back of the man's head. I recall thinking it odd that this man was able to shoot himself directly in the back of his head. As I continued to do chest compressions with my left hand, Brian encouraged me to place one of my right fingers at the wound, perhaps to teach me, maybe just to gross me out, but it struck me that I wasn't as traumatized by the action as I thought I'd be.

Shortly thereafter, in 2000, when I was asked to join the Victim Services Crisis Team, it didn't take me long to realize just how much exposure the ambulance rides had given me and what excellent preparation those calls had been for my first experiences with the police department and with handling traumatic, crisis situations.

Now, surely, I could handle the memorial services and graveside ceremonies without feeling much effect.

* * *

The funeral service for Officer Rodney Kendricks was held on Wednesday, July 11, 2001, at Trinity Church in Lubbock, Texas.

For 12 years, Officer Kendricks had faithfully served the police department, joining the force in May of 1989, and eventually transferring to the motorcycle unit in April of 2000. On Sunday, July 8, 2001, he died at the age of 33 as a result of injuries suffered in an accident while on duty.

The service was extremely emotional, with "final call" being the roughest part. I'd learned, and later experienced, the lifeline that the radio and the dispatcher on the other end were to officers. If Dispatch called an officer and there was no answer, it would start to raise concern. If called a second time and no answer, this was a problem and could indicate they needed help. Soon the dispatcher would be considering how to find out where they were and what to do about their radio silence.

Introduction

The "final call" in this funeral service began when an assistant police chief turned on a portable radio, and everyone present could hear Dispatch calling out Rodney's number. I sat there thinking of the first time when I had learned how to call in at the end of my shift and report, "10-42," indicating that I was done with my job and I was going home. I soon discovered that if Dispatch ever called me and I didn't answer, every officer on duty would immediately tune in. If Dispatch called me a second time and I still didn't answer, they'd be ready to move into action.

Now, at the end of the service, a radio was turned on, and a dispatcher's voice could be heard calling out Officer Kendricks's number the first time.

There was silence. Then crying grew louder.

Dispatch called his number again.

The weeping grew louder.

Dispatch called Officer Kendricks's unit number a third time.

A few seconds later, after radio silence, knowing there would be no answer, Dispatch quietly announced: "Five-twelve is 10-42."

Officer Rodney Kendricks had ended his tour of duty.

After the service, the motorcycle division of the Lubbock Police Department escorted Rodney's body from the church in Lubbock to the Sunset Memorial Park in Odessa, Texas, two hours away, for burial.

As I thought about the service that day, I realized that it had been exceptionally stirring—at moments, agonizing—and for me, totally unexpected. It affected me more than I had thought possible.

Then, two days later, on Friday, July 13, 2001, the Lubbock Police Department suffered another personal and devastating loss. Sergeant Kevin Cox was also killed in the line of duty.

Unbelievably, while still reeling from Rodney's death, within just a few days we were all back in the very same sanctuary. Kevin's funeral was held on Tuesday, July 17, also at Trinity Church, where 2,000 people gathered to pay their respects.

The thirty-eight-year-old Cox had joined the force in 1985 and eventually became a patrol supervisor who also served on the SWAT team. This team was called out on Friday, July 13, to a South Lubbock home where Sergeant Cox was then shot and killed when he and five other SWAT members executed a "break-and-rake" on a window. He was pronounced dead at the hospital approximately 30 minutes later.

This ceremony was also poignant, profound, moving, and gave me the sense that I was on hallowed ground. The format was the same as Rodney's funeral—another funeral too soon.

Once again, at the end of the church service, the crowd listened to the police dispatcher's voice calling out for Kevin's unit number once . . . then twice . . . then three times.

There was no response,

Only the sound of mournful cries.

Dispatch then quietly declared, "Sergeant Cox is 10-42."

Sergeant Kevin Cox was going home.

* * *

In that moment, the Law Enforcement Oath of Honor was personally meaningful to me. I was proud to be associated with the Lubbock Police Department and set a course to serve the community of Lubbock and assist the brave men and women who continuously and literally lay down their lives in service for all.

CHAPTER ONE
THE JOB THAT FOUND ME

"Choose a job you love, and you will never have to work a day in your life."

—Confucius

The law enforcement community is a close-knit community and suspect of outsiders, especially crack dealers and mental health professionals. Early on, walking the halls of the police department, I could feel and even see the disapproval and resentment of my presence. There were the brief nods of acknowledgment, but I was often aware of an instantaneous urge to flip me off.

Here I was, walking through the police department of Lubbock, and I suspected there were already three charges held against me.

Number one—This was Texas…and I was *not* from Texas. I had lived most of my life in Bellevue, Washington—the largest suburb of Seattle, and a city that manages to rank decisively liberal on any political survey. Lubbock, on the other hand, was like every other good town in Texas—die-hard conservative, and where almost everyone owned a gun. As for me, I grew up climbing trees and mountains; and the closest thing to a weapon I had ever used was an oar, paddling around Lake Washington.

Number two—I didn't have any background in the military or law enforcement; I toted a degree in Bible, another in Youth and Family Ministry, and a third in Community Counseling. Currently, I was teaching psychology at a private, Christian university.

Eleven years earlier, in 1989, I had come to West Texas to attend college. For a while, I wasn't sure I had made the right decision. I distinctly remember this huge wave of dread hitting me as I drove down from Seattle, from beautiful mountains and lakes, to these flatlands. The dread reached its pinnacle during the last two-hour drive south from Amarillo to Lubbock. Outside my car window, I witnessed this flat…brown…windy…dust bowl-like…no-man's land at the center of what they called the South Plains—and I thought, *what have I done! I will never get through this; this place is like the surface of the moon.* Finally, I arrived in the "Hub City"—one hundred miles from anywhere.

The culture shock I went through was a surprise because I didn't expect such a difference between these two states, but while the land looked barren and dry, I discovered that most of the people were anything but drab and lifeless. On the contrary, everyone here was open and friendly, asking me, a stranger, how I was doing—it was very odd. So, I decided to respond in kind, because it seemed everyone wanted to be my friend. Unfortunately, that meant people got to experience my sarcastic sense of humor. It didn't sit too well with anyone who really wasn't interested in hearing much more than, "I'm fine, and you?" Still, people were generally nicer than what I was now experiencing in the police department halls.

Which brings me to the third offense, a felony—I was not a police officer. I was one of those crazy, mental health types who probably thought he could fix anybody in the world with a big hug.

I was well aware that police officers are usually the no-touchy-feely, I-can-deal-with-my-own-stuff, psychological-armor-wearing, taught-to-put-bad-guys-in-jail kind of people. Couple all of that with the determination to be a tight-knit community, and it's not hard to figure out that a volunteer mental health professional (MHP) would probably have a hard time being accepted or utilized. Although I was expecting a slightly warmer welcome, I didn't blame them for their attitude. MHPs can be CRA-ZY! Somehow, though, I resolved to demonstrate that something new and suspect could actually be beneficial.

In the year 2000, when I was attending church one Sunday morning, the police chief's secretary, Mary McGuire, approached me to ask if I'd be interested in joining a newly forming group of mental health counselors—what they were calling the Victim Services Crisis Team (VSCT).

The chief of the Lubbock Police Department had determined that his officers were spending too much time dealing with non-police issues when answering calls, especially domestic-related disputes where no assault had occurred and no arrest was warranted—homes where people simply needed to work out some issues with one another. The chief felt that if a few counselor-types could handle these emotionally charged situations, his officers could get back to doing what they were supposed to do. I eventually understood that while some other police departments had trained their officers to handle mental health or crisis intervention issues, or perhaps paired a police officer trained in mental health to work with a MHP while on patrol, our crisis counseling unit would be unique in that we would serve as two MHPs riding and working together in an unmarked police car.

And so, I showed up on July 7, 2000, along with about 12 other volunteers, to begin training. For the next two weeks, we reviewed the responsibilities and operation of the police department, as well as the organization and management of the judicial system. We learned how to operate a city car, drive defensively, how to yell for help on a radio, how to find an address anywhere in the city, and how to operate the computer to look up information about the calls to which officers were being dispatched (call sheets). We were taught basic crisis intervention techniques—how to stabilize a situation, how to stay safe, and the importance of staying calm. On one very hot day, we spent significant time practicing the art of properly installing a child seat in a city car in case we ever needed to transport children to another location. We went over the protocol of transporting adults as well.

Before we started our first shift, we were told that we should respond to a scene whenever we received a call or a page via Dispatch, from any one of the three hundred officers who determined that a person like me, with a background in mental health, would be of assistance in a crisis situation that already involved police action and/or protection.

We were also informed, however, that officers are naturally suspicious, especially of new programs, new people, and "mental health types." We should expect some odd looks and resistance. (Check!) Nevertheless, I was excited to give this crisis-intervention-with-the-police- department-thing a try, and was willing to stay the course, even if it took a long time to gain their acceptance and trust.

The police chief wanted the counselors to volunteer at least one shift per month, on a Friday or Saturday from 7:00 p.m. to 2:00 a.m. And because I had just earned a master's degree in counseling and spent some time riding along with ambulance and emergency medical helicopter crews, I felt fairly prepared for whatever we'd be facing.

My first shift began on Friday, July 21, when I joined my partner, Debbie Frapp, who was also the director of Contact Lubbock—a suicide referral hotline. She had a wealth of knowledge of agencies in town and would be our own excellent referral system.

That evening, the two of us showed up at the police department, signed in, picked up a radio and city car, and we cruised around, waiting for an officer or two to call us to accompany them. Our supervisor was Sergeant Mark Wims, who had attended our training. He was very cordial, quickly communicated to the other officers who we were, and instructed them to give us a call and be open to our help. And over the next seven hours, we were actually called to assist with four incidents. I remember one call was canceled while we were en route, and two of the other calls, not surprisingly, were domestic-related. We spent one hour with a couple who had been arguing—loudly—but it was nothing serious. I did my marriage and therapy thing, and Debbie did her referral thing. At the end of the shift, we each submitted two reports for our four calls.

I was impressed and pleasantly surprised that four police officers had contacted us through radio dispatch, provided an address, and asked us to assist. They were able to go back into service while we did our thing, which was helpful for the department.

It was not our intention to show the cops how important we were, neither did we think we had anything to teach them. On the contrary, we were going to get quite the education about that one percent of society that most people don't know exists. During one particular callout, my education included an interesting lesson when I walked into a house and heard an officer talking to a man and his wife about shooting an intruder.

Several hours earlier, in the middle of the night, a drunken college student had broken through their sliding glass door. And so, they did what every stereotypical Texas homeowner would do—the man grabbed his .38 from the nightstand and his wife picked up her revolver. After warning the young man a number of times to leave the premises, they felt they had no other choice but to shoot. Then they dialed 911. When I was called in to help the obviously shaken couple, I could hear one of the officers lecturing, almost criticizing this man and woman on the dangers of crossfire. (Only in Texas!)

All joking aside, I consider Lubbock a great place to live and work. With a population of about 250,000 (as of 2015), the city still has a small-town feel and I can usually travel from one part to any other in 15 minutes or less. It's the central hub for much of west Texas and eastern New Mexico, and touts an interesting combination as both a college town (home to Texas Tech University and Lubbock Christian University, where I teach) and a family-oriented place. Lubbock is also the home of two major hospitals, where I spend time with a number of victims: Covenant Hospital as well as University Medical Center, which also serves as the primary teaching hospital for Texas Tech University Health Sciences Center, and is the only Level I Trauma Center in the region. I commented earlier about the dry and barren land, but the truth is, there are plenty of trees and greenery. Shrubbery does grow in some parts instead of cotton, and not everyone is a cowboy. Even so, there are lots of horses and cattle, and agriculture is big, as denoted by the noon agribusiness report on the AM dial.

Since I arrived in Lubbock years ago to attend college, I've made great friends and am convinced that the people are the nicest anywhere. Still, for those first few years with the police department, there was nothing like having my every interaction, every call, and every comment scrutinized. And just like any other good and efficient operation, these officers talked to one another—one screw-up, and the entire force knew within seconds. But to be fair, when I would calmly handle a tough call under pressure, or did something that surprised everyone, or was in some way helpful, the same reaction held true.

I recall when a desk sergeant took an opportunity to give me a hard time for "being a liberal" in front of a bunch of people. Remember, I'm a professor, a MHP, *and* from Seattle. I knew my reply would be on trial. The fact is, however, I'm not a liberal and said so truthfully while shooting back with some humor and sarcasm.

By the time the end of my first year as a volunteer rolled around, I had also been asked to be part of a new intervention team and attend CISM (Critical Incident Stress Management) training. With my background in counseling, I thought it was the perfect fit. Two other MHPs and I joined four police officers and learned how to help their peers talk about and cope with traumatic experiences associated with their work. Soon after that training, I was likewise recruited to attend training for negotiators with the SWAT team.

All in all, during that first twelve months, I can say that I experienced a pretty good dose of adrenaline. I'd been involved with a few traffic accidents, a number of domestic disputes, a couple of suicides, a sexual assault, and a runaway child call. I learned that being honest, forthright, understanding, and frank were all good characteristics to possess (thanks, Mom and Dad!). I'd also become more acquainted with the emergency services culture. These people had been hard to get to know; yet they were professional, close-knit, and hilarious at times (if you don't mind the darker gallows humor), and they loved their work—most of the time.

This group was definitely in the business of helping others, and being on the job most every day, they were the answer to many a prayer. Perhaps that's why, when it came time to seek help for themselves, it wasn't something that came easily. Regardless, the need to seek help could arise at any moment . . . as the entire department would soon discover.

CHAPTER TWO
OFFICER DOWN

"Blessed are those who mourn, for they shall be comforted."
—Matthew 5:4 (NASB)

The police supervisor in charge of the motorcycle division understood that his officers were hurting. They were having a hard time dealing with the death of a fellow comrade, and the officer in charge felt they needed some help. When he happened to mention the seriousness of the situation to Mary McGuire, he wasn't aware that we had just recently formed a CISM (Critical Incident Stress Management) team and that we were in the midst of finalizing policies and procedures.

A week before, on Monday, July 2, 2001, Officer Rodney Kendricks, a motorcycle officer, had been accidentally hit by another vehicle as he was escorting a funeral procession through the city. As part of his responsibilities during a procession, he and other motor squad officers would halt traffic at each intersection to allow the vehicles following the hearse to pass through. Once all other vehicles not associated with the procession had completely stopped to yield the right of way, an officer would then leapfrog ahead of the procession to block off the next intersection. Unfortunately, because of a curve in the road, neither Officer Kendricks, who was moving ahead of the procession, nor the driver coming in the opposite direction saw each other in time to avoid a collision in the middle turn lane. It was a bad day.

Kendricks survived a few more days in the hospital. Sadly, his injuries were too critical to overcome and he passed away on Sunday, July 8. Now, instead of Officer Kendricks protecting and serving a grieving entourage, he was the one who would be guarded by his fellow officers and accompanied to his final resting place.

On Monday, July 9, as a member of the newly formed CISM team, I was asked to conduct a "defusing" with the motor squad. It seemed to be a big deal that our fledgling CISM team was asked for help, so we decided to set up the short meeting for the motor squad where they would have an opportunity to discuss the traumatic event, psychologically process it, and in turn, begin to cope with the loss of their friend.

This was my second time leading such a group. The first occasion was with a group of police officers that had been called to the hospital emergency room after a prison inmate had taken two ER nurses hostage. The prisoner surrendered, but afterwards, the police learned that he had sexually assaulted the nurses. This was quite distressing to the officers, who were already angry with the prison guards for abandoning their prisoner when the guards thought he had taken possession of a gun. The weapon turned out to be a black hairbrush, modified to look like a handgun. The officers' anger was compounded when an armed prison guard was observed holding his revolver like a dead rat, asking if someone could help him uncock his weapon.

The circumstances surrounding that first group meeting were quite different than the ones we now faced. Both involved high stakes; however, I considered this meeting to be much more difficult because this traumatic event involved the injury and death of a coworker. When bad things happen to strangers, it's easier to maintain a professional distance, which helps emergency services workers function effectively. But when the patient you are transporting in an ambulance is wearing the same uniform you are, you can't help but feel the danger looking over your own shoulder and sizing you up as well—"There but for the grace of God go I."[1] There but for the grace of God go I. This feeling, coupled with the grief associated with the loss of a friend, dramatically changed the tenor of this meeting.

All things considered, the meeting went well, technically. Afterward, I hoped the seven attending officers derived some small benefit. We could have conducted a debriefing (a longer and psychologically in-depth group meeting), but we didn't want the officers to take off their psychological armor just yet. In a few days, they would need to attend the funeral and escort the procession two hours away to a cemetery in Odessa, Officer Kendrick's hometown. This would be an extremely long and daunting endeavor. So, we waited a few more days.

On Tuesday, July 10, two days after Rodney's death, I attended the wake. The following day, July 11, I would attend his funeral. At the conclusion of the service, I was moved by the squad of motorcycle officers pulling away from the church in Lubbock. I remember saying to one of my coworkers, "It just can't get any worse than this," something I would soon regret saying.

Two days later, on Friday, July 13, as I was driving home from my teaching gig, I was diverted by the police, who had set up a barricade. Consequently, I was forced to take a different route home. I'd never seen this before and was very interested in what the cops might be up to.

As soon as I walked into my house, I turned on the TV news and discovered that the department had initiated a SWAT callout. I later

---

1   A paraphrase of First Corinthians 15:10: "But by the grace of God I am what I am, and His grace toward me was not in vain…" (NKJV) Origin of the paraphrase has been attributed to various clerics of the 16th-18th centuries, including John Bradford, Richard Baxter, John Newton, and Philip Neri.

learned that one of the other MHPs on our crisis team had been called to go to the scene where a man had barricaded himself in his own house, located in a residential neighborhood close to the main thoroughfare I used to get home from work.

Later that afternoon, Mary McGuire called me. "Andy," she said, "we need you to come down to the police department. Kevin Cox has been killed." Within minutes I was out the door, realizing again that I wasn't being called by the police to help a civilian, but to help the police themselves.

At the station I found out what happened. Earlier that day, a woman had called 911 claiming her husband was in their front yard, burning their clothes, furniture, and other personal items. He was distraught and had made comments to someone about suicide.

When two patrol officers reported to the scene, the guy who was doing the burning ran inside, while his wife ran out, telling the officers her husband owned some guns. For the next four hours, a standoff ensued. Police negotiators attempted to call the subject 39 times by phone, but never received an answer. Eventually, a six-member SWAT Rescue team moved in to break a window to prepare for the option of using tear gas. This maneuver would also let the man inside know that this situation was serious, and hopefully motivate him to answer the negotiator's calls.

As the officers approached the window they called out, "Police! Police!" They performed the break-and-rake and then held their position. Suddenly there was a boom, and an officer went down. A second officer jumped out of the way, went down to the ground, and in the process, lost his helmet. While other team members took cover, another officer stepped across the downed officer, and with an MP-5, he fired through the window.

In the midst of all the chaos, SWAT called for cover fire in order to facilitate an officer rescue. The shooting continued while the team, trying to manage all their gear, awkwardly attempted to pick up the downed officer and drag him to the Emergency Rescue Vehicle (an armored personnel carrier). They weren't having an easy time of it.

Sergeant Kevin Cox was the officer who was down. He was pronounced dead at University Medical Center about 30 minutes later. Another officer, Johnny Hutson, was injured as well. His head had been grazed by a bullet in the same gunfire that killed Sergeant Cox.

Sergeant Ross Hester was the primary negotiator that day who had called 39 times without anyone answering. During the break-and-rake, and on the 40th ring of the 40th call, the man inside answered because he was upset that his window was being broken. Then gunfire erupted. After the officer rescue, the man inside informed Sergeant Hester he had been shot in the butt and was worried that he would be killed. Sergeant Hester let him know how he needed to come out of the house so he would not be hurt. When he did not come out, police filled his house with copious amounts of chemical agent. He finally came out and was taken into custody without incident.

After I learned these details, an assistant police chief pulled me aside to say that he was very concerned about his people. A complement of 300 officers was still reeling from the death of Kendricks a few days ago, and now this had happened. At that very moment, the SWAT team was in the briefing room, writing reports and taking care of their equipment, and the chief wanted someone trained in CISM to help them. Although other police officers in the department had also been trained in this intervention, the fact that they personally knew and worked with Kevin meant that, understandably, they should not conduct such a meeting. My partner, Debbie, likewise knew Kevin. So under these circumstances, the chief semi-asked, semi-ordered, "Go on in there and see what you can do to help them out."

I had a multitude of concerns about just "winging it" through some spur-of-the moment counseling session, but I didn't feel this was a good time to educate the chief on how CISM was supposed to work or how it should be deployed. Rather, it was a time to simply say, "Yes, sir."

As I talked with Debbie prior to entering the briefing room, the hazards associated with what we were about to do were weighing heavily upon me. I mentioned the need for brevity, and Debbie agreed. I decided to conduct a quick demobilization, talk about a few coping measures, and mention something about how to transition from a traumatic experience at work to going home. I was very nervous. I felt as if we were entering hallowed ground and that even our mere presence was disrespectful. Walking down the hall, I specifically prayed, "Oh God, help me to not make this worse."

Just about the time we entered the room, another professional counselor joined us. I didn't know her, and I wasn't sure what she was doing there; nevertheless, I tried to be optimistic and assume her presence would be helpful. Yet to be honest, I was anxious about someone just showing up to help without warning.

As the three of us entered the room and took a seat at the front, I could feel the icy silence. I had to force myself to look into the tired eyes and sweaty faces of those officers whose friend had just died, and I thought, *what could I offer these men? What on earth could be helpful to them at a time like this?*

Soon, someone entered the room and said, "This guy is here to help you." Then he turned and walked out. I was pretty sure these officers weren't about guys like me or really big on my kind of help. And my assumptions were thrown back at me by looks that said, "Get the hell out."

There was nothing else to do but start.

"Hi, my name is Andy Young. I'm with the CISM team…."

Sprinting through what I had momentarily practiced, I mentioned that they might have trouble sleeping, or become irritable, or lose their appetite. I recommended they might want to drink lots of water, eat even if they didn't feel like it, make sure to keep talking to family and friends, and just…take care of each other.

In conclusion, I said, "We'll probably set up a meeting at a later date." Then I tried to throw out a little encouragement with something along the lines of, "You'll all get through this."

It took all of 45 seconds and fell far short of what I really wanted to give these men.

When one of the officers realized I had stopped talking, he glared at me through the cold silence and irritably said, "Are you done?"

I nodded.

He continued, "Then I need all non-sworn personnel to exit this room." All of my fears were realized in that moment, as the three of us were the only non-sworn personnel in the room. In other words, I heard him say loud and clear, "Get the h--- out."

Immediately, Debbie and I stepped out into the hall. The other lady disappeared and almost at once, one of the assistant chiefs said to me, "Andy, they need you guys up at the hospital—in the emergency room."

I quickly acquired a city car, and Debbie and I made our way across town. When we walked into the hospital, we were immediately briefed by one of the men in a group of assistant chiefs and command staff.

"Andy, I don't know what's going on," he said, "but one of the officers who was at the scene today is really upset. He keeps saying, 'I killed Kevin.' "

As these commanders continued to talk, I learned that during the standoff, the officer claiming to have shot Kevin had been posted across the street and set up as part of the rifle team. Everyone was aware that earlier that day he had covered the window where the six-member SWAT team had conducted the brake-and-rake. The chiefs didn't know exactly what had happened, but they were convinced, after looking at the news tape and talking with other on-site personnel, that this officer couldn't have killed Kevin. In the meantime, they were really confused as to why he was claiming to be responsible.

The assistant chief finally said, "We're hoping you can go in there and try to help him."

Per his instructions, Debbie and I entered the room in the ER, introduced ourselves to the officer, and let him know we were there for him. The officer was obviously very distraught and had little to say. I tried to ask a few questions and get more of a conversation going, but he just wasn't up to talking. Even so, we stayed with him for a while and made sure he knew how to contact us.

Later I learned that this policeman's regular assignment was that of a motorcycle officer. Earlier in the week, he had lost his friend and coworker in the line of duty and had escorted the hearse just two days ago. Today he had been assigned to the SWAT team as a sniper, and now he felt he was responsible for an officer's death.

When we left the hospital, we went directly to his house to speak with his wife and prepare her for her husband's release from the ER. We tried to discuss the possibility of depression and suicide because her husband believed he'd just killed his friend. This conversation was very confusing to her, as was everything else about the day. We did our best, made sure that officers would be checking on the family, and mentioned that we would follow up with the family the next day.

When I returned to the police department, it became clear to me that I needed to seek assistance from our CISM trainer, a man named Vaughn Donaldson, who had presented the stress management course to our department during the previous months. When I called him later that Friday evening, he offered to travel from Midland to Lubbock the very next morning and promised to bring along some help.

On the evening of Saturday, July 14, a CISM-trained SWAT officer (Vaughn) and I conducted a psychological debriefing for the entire SWAT team as well as the negotiators who had been involved with the incident. This meeting gave about 35 officers an opportunity to mentally and emotionally process the tragic callout. I couldn't have been more relieved for Vaughn's help or more grateful for this valuable experience.

For over three hours, Vaughn asked all types of questions that helped the officers talk about the experience (e.g., "Tell us what happened from your perspective throughout this incident? What was the worst part?"). It was a difficult meeting. The officer who claimed to have shot Kevin also attended, but was quiet the entire time. Obviously, the weight of the world was upon him. I'm not sure if any other officer knew what he had been saying, but no one was pointing a finger. All conversations reflected the assumption that the man inside the house had killed Kevin. In any case, the meeting seemed to be productive, giving people a chance to talk through what had happened and how they felt.

This assistance continued during the next few days as Vaughn helped us to schedule, staff, announce, and conduct ten debriefings, so that every officer within the department would have an opportunity to attend. We divided the groups based on their exposure to the SWAT callout. After the first debriefing with all SWAT officers and negotiators, we held another meeting for the officers on the perimeter of the callout, another for the motorcycle squad (which included the incident regarding Officer Rodney Kendrick's accident and death), a debriefing for dispatchers, one for officers on duty that day, a meeting for the investigators and detectives who were on scene afterwards, a debriefing for officer spouses, and an additional meeting for other squads who were grieving Kevin as well.

Of the many meetings we held that week, one in particular stands out—the debriefing with patrol officers who initially responded to the callout and were on the perimeter. Those of us conducting this debriefing (CISM-trained officers from DPS and other law enforcement agencies that came in to assist) met early to get to know each other and discuss how to handle this meeting, especially because there was a chance a captain would be in attendance. Usually, and per our CISM training, command staff and supervisors are expected to meet separately from officers so that their presence will not cause participants to hold back.

We discussed what we would do if this captain attended, and agreed that a DPS (Department of Public Safety) state trooper would probably ask the captain to leave, especially since the captain hadn't been on scene that day. Unfortunately, this captain attended and the trooper did not ask him to leave. It was obvious that his presence provoked the officers to speak carefully. At one point, one of the officers began to defend his decisions made that day, and we wondered if the captain's attendance was about finding blame or searching for error among his troops. We recognized afterward that this meeting had probably been a waste of everyone's time.

Meanwhile, in the midst of the many debriefings, a second funeral was scheduled and held on Tuesday, July 17, 2001, in honor of Sergeant Kevin Cox—just six days after the ceremonies had been conducted for Officer Kendricks. We were having another funeral.

Once again, it was a profound experience to be a part of the church ceremony and extremely moving to witness the SWAT team surround the casket and escort the hearse from the church to the graveside. As I walked out of the church, I noticed Aerocare's helicopter hovering overhead and likewise escorting the funeral procession. Public safety workers from more than 20 surrounding agencies attended the ceremonies as well, including a unit from Dallas and one from New Mexico.

During the drive from the church to the cemetery, I was overwhelmed as I beheld this long stretch of people—thousands of men, women, and children solemnly standing for seven miles alongside streets and highways, paying their respects, in the 100-degree heat. Fire truck after fire truck was parked along the way, and all types of emergency services personnel were standing at attention and saluting. The display of respect choked me up more than anything else that day.

Later, while standing at the gravesite, I noticed that a second helicopter, one from the Texas Department of Public Safety, had joined the chopper from AeroCare. After about 30 minutes, both of them gently peeled away. Then, remarkably, as the bagpipes played, "Amazing Grace," a large hawk took their place and floated above us for several more minutes. Eventually, the sound of the hymn faded as the piper marched off between the graves.

At the end of the ceremony, with all uniformed personnel lined up and standing at salute, seven honor guards fired three successive shots. Then a solitary bugler played the mournful sound of "Taps." I lingered until it was time to walk to my car.

* * *

The next day, on Wednesday, July 18, 2001, I read an article entitled, "Farewell to a Servant" in the *Lubbock Avalanche-Journal* and learned that the day before, investigators had spent their fourth day at the crime scene, continuing their investigation. At times, they could only stay in the house for five-minute shifts. They were wearing hazmat suits because of the tear gas and they were in the 120 degree heat of the house. In addition, the gunman was supposed to be released from the hospital. He had been charged with capital murder with bond set at one million dollars.

Then two days later on Friday, July 20, detectives of the Lubbock Police Department made an announcement. No functional guns had been found in the house. Moreover, it was determined the gunshot that had killed Kevin had come from a sniper rifle which had first penetrated another officer's helmet. Consequently, the DA's office dismissed the charges against the homeowner and he was released.

Media coverage prior to this time had been intense; but now, with the release of this new revelation, the story reached a fever pitch. There was a lot of drama, questioning, and hand-wringing over the course of the next few weeks, all of which re-traumatized those closely associated with this callout.

On Sunday, July 22, the chief of police, who was out of town during the callout, was put on administrative leave. Soon, though, politics and forces brought to bear by the media, being what they are, eventually led to his dismissal as well as the demotion of the assistant chief in charge that day. Members of the SWAT team who had requested or provided cover fire were no longer on the team. The rifle team officer who accidentally discharged his rifle lost his job.

Moreover, a few officers were mandated to see city-sanctioned counselors, which did not go well. We learned that not all MHPs are created equal and not every counselor is able to help with law enforcement situations. I learned a lot about trying to provide CISM services under the most difficult circumstances. As one of my first CISM interventions after being trained, this was a rough way to get introduced to this line of work.

After the dust settled, everyone was reeling with grief. Morale could not have been lower, especially among those SWAT officers who were disciplined and/or let go from the SWAT team. What began as a difficult SWAT callout, was now an impossible nightmare. The facts changed from the bad guy killing Sergeant Cox to another officer accidentally killing Sergeant Cox. This made two traumatizing incidents out of one, and it seemed as if the devastation that had begun the week before Rodney's death would never end.

CHAPTER THREE
THE NEGOTIATION

> *"I have heard that we are spirits having a human experience. Perhaps those of us who have no conscience are dark spirits having a human experience."*
> —P.A. Speers

I slowly turned over and forced myself up out of bed. Standing there for just a second, I tried to wake up, but was still struggling as I half-stumbled, half-hurried through the dark to the living room and our home phone.

I thought, *why does the phone have to sound so intense in the middle of the night?* Then it rang another time, and I grabbed the receiver before it had a chance to wake my neighbors or split my skull.

"Hello?" I answered, trying to sound like I had not been sleeping at three o'clock in the morning.

"This is Officer So-and-So with the Lubbock Police Department. Is this Andy Young?"

"Uh, yeah"...*I think so.*

"Chief McGuire asked me to call you. There's a guy who's barricaded himself inside a house, and he's hollerin' for a priest and a counselor. Here's his number...We need you to call him and keep him busy while SWAT gets set up."

Say what? Who is this?

Now, I started to wake up.

After about six months of volunteering as a mental health counselor with the police department and helping a number of victims in various emergency situations, I'd been asked to attend training for SWAT negotiators and become a member of the team. But that training hadn't happened yet, nor had I been to any team meetings or trainings. Even so, it seemed that someone thought it was a good idea to put me in the hot seat at this crazy hour of the night and keep this guy distracted.

Fortunately, my own adrenaline was now helping me to keep my eyes open, and I did what all good counselors would do in a situation like this—paraphrase.

"So...let me get this right. This guy has barricaded himself?"

"Yeah."

"And he wants to talk to a priest or counselor?"

"Uh-huh."

"And you want me to call him and keep him busy while SWAT gets set up."

"That's right."

"Okay." So I wrote the number down.

As soon as I hung up the phone, I picked it back up and immediately dialed the number, even though I wasn't sure what to do.

After a ring or two, some guy answered. And this guy was definitely wide-awake.

"HELLO!" he barked.

In the background, I could hear this dark, angry-techno music pounding away. After I introduced myself and deftly said, "I understand you'd like to speak with a counselor," he spouted "What d'ya want!"

Obviously, this guy was agitated, and I assumed that he'd probably been drinking.

Why am I doing this? I wondered.

"Hi, my name is Andy. I understand you want to talk to a counselor tonight. Can you tell me what's going on tonight?"

"What?!"

Taking a breath, I began one more time.

"My name is Andy. The police gave me your phone number. I understand you want to speak with a counselor. Is there something I can help you with?"

"Where'd you get your license from!?" he snapped.

"Sorry?"

"I saiiiid...where'd you get your f---in' license from?"

I still had no idea what this guy was asking me or what was happening here; even so, I took a stab at answering his question.

"Well...I...I have a national license. I'm a...national certified counselor..."

"Whaaat?! I said...WHERE'D YOU GET YOUR F---IN' LICENSE FROM?"

What does this guy want me to say?

"Well...uh...I got a license from the state of Texas."

"No, no! I want to know where you got your f---in' license from... I'm not talking 'bout your f---in'...f---in'...I want to know about the f---in'...f---in'..."

So, I took another shot at it.

"Well, I went to school...got a license...blah-blah-blah...supervisor...took a test...blah-blah-blah...license...state of Texas...blah-blah-blah...another test...another license..."

"No-uh!...I want to know...where'd ya get your...f---in'...f---in'...f---in'..."

Then I heard him say, "I want to talk to someone who knows what they're f---in' doin'."

And he hung up.

I had no idea what had just happened, and I was extremely confused as I stood there reviewing in my mind this absurd circumstance and pseudo-conversation. But, since there was nothing else I could do, I went back to bed.

The thought to dial 911 didn't occur to me. Dialing 911 was for emergencies, and I didn't know what to call this. The guy had just f-bombed me for a minute—and that was it. Furthermore, I didn't have a phone number for the officer who had called me, and I had no idea how to contact him (this was in the days before everyday use of cell phones). And…well…I just went back to bed.

Ten minutes later, the phone rang again. Again, I went out to the living room—this time with a little more speed and direction—and I picked up the phone.

"Hello?"

"Lubbock Police."

"Yeah?" I answered, thinking, *Thank God, the cops are calling me back.*

"You guys should know that the door's not grounded."

What?! Oh no, this isn't the Lubbock Police. It's the bad guy calling me back.

"I put C-4 in the walls and connected explosives to the door…."

As he continued to talk, I thought to myself, *this guy wasn't identifying himself as the Lubbock Police; he was asking me if I was the police. And he heard me say, "Yeah." I've just told this barricaded angry man that he's talking to the Lubbock Police. Great, now I've impersonated the police—real nice.*

Then it really hit me. Even though I didn't have caller ID in 2001 when this call came in, this guy evidently did. And now, he had my home phone number.

And did he just say, "The door's not grounded"?

Even as I was realizing the identity confusion between us, he was continuing to rattle on about explosives planted in the walls and front doors not being grounded—and some other stuff I had never heard before.

I thought I'd better start paying attention.

"What do you mean?" I interrupted.

"I put C-4 in the walls … connected explosives to the door … got them wired to the doorframe. Tell your guys not to come through the door because it's not grounded."

I was as confused as ever but felt like saying, "There you go. This makes perfect sense. And of course, they taught me all sorts of things in counselor school about explosive ordinance disarming, and disposal, and…"

At this point, the best I could do was to use my basic counselor's skill—repeat everything back to him. Fortunately, he seemed to be calmer than he had been during our first phone call, and he was decent enough to confirm my paraphrase.

Then it seemed as though he had run out of things to say.

"So…" I asked, "Would you like to talk about what's goin' on tonight?"

Click.

He hung up again. This sounded bad and my mind was racing. Still, I didn't know what to do. I was new to this negotiating thing, and I had no idea whom to call. So…

I went back to bed.

But, no…I didn't go to sleep; only a psychopath could do that. I just couldn't find a way to turn off my mind, and I couldn't stop trying to figure out what to do with this new information. Several minutes later, as I was having visions of city blocks blowing up, the phone rang again.

Oh man, I hope this guy doesn't expect me to be Lubbock Police.

I picked up the phone like it was contaminated.

"Hello?" I said with some fear and trepidation.

"Hey Andy, this is Officer So-and-So. I'm checkin' in to see how it went with the…"

Before he finished the sentence, I began to pour out the details as coherently and as quickly as possible. At times, the officer seemed a little confused by my description, and every couple of phrases he would stop me to say, "Now, let me get this straight." Eventually, though, he seemed to make sense of everything and we ended our conversation.

When I hung up the phone for the fourth time, I went back to bed, but still couldn't sleep. I figured that I had completely failed. Even though the phone stopped ringing, I spent the rest of the night trying to figure out what had just happened.

The next day, I learned the whole story. The angry, barricaded subject was a college student who had been drinking and taking Accutane (a powerful drug used to treat acne, but in rare instances, can cause a person to become suicidal and/or homicidal). I also learned that a guy asking to talk to a priest is rarely a good sign. I'm really glad I didn't know that when I agreed to make the call.

The SWAT team eventually drove a tank with a battering ram through this guy's living room window. Then they swept out the window and went in to arrest him. No explosives were ever found in the wall. In addition, I discovered that when this guy first called the police earlier that night, he decided to threaten the officer answering the phone with a countdown.

Sergeant Robert Mayne listened as the young man started to count backwards from ten to one in German: zehn…neun…acht…sieben…sechs…fünf…vier…drei…zwei…eins.

Later, during the call, he counted down from ten to one in Spanish: diez…nueve…ocho…siete…seis…cinco…cuatro…tres…dos…uno. And again, the sergeant listened.

Then the guy wanted to show off his language skills in French. But this time, as soon as he began, Sergeant Mayne decided to join him: dix, (deese)…neuf (nurf)…huit (wheet)…sept (set)…six (seese)…cinq (sank)…quatre (kat)…trois (twah)…deux (duhr)…un (uhn).

At that point, the caller became even more irritated and hung up the phone. Guess he was driven to pretend to have explosives in his house because of Sgt. Mayne's counting help.

As I've reminisced and retold this story, I've laughed at my own inexperience and embarrassment during what was my first official SWAT callout. I'll also add that not long after this incident in 2001, I began training with the negotiating team and was added to that team as a consultant. In the meantime, I continued serving as a crisis counselor and on our CISM team.

The Negotiation

* * *

Two years and many calls later, on November 21, 2003, a call came in from the south-central part of the city. The police learned that a man, a naked man, was holding a woman hostage in her apartment.

As soon as I heard "a naked man," I immediately remembered what I'd learned through personal research on deadly calls for police officers. At first, when many people (including myself), hear of someone streaking through a downtown park or across the field of a ball stadium, we grin and think, *Okay, I want to see this. But, nah...I don't want to see this. But, yeah, I want to see this.* It does sound funny. However, it is a serious situation and potentially deadly.

I remember one particular call. I had been cruising around in one of the department cars, working a 7:00 p.m. to 2:00 a.m. shift, when I heard a call come over the radio, "Naked man on a roof . . . " Of course, I got there as soon as I could.

Even though it was 30 degrees outside, sure enough, "naked man" was walking around on a roof, engaged in an all-out conversation with his God. I also noticed that along with a crowd of neighbors, a fire truck, four firefighters, an EMS (emergency medical services) pickup truck, an ambulance, and three patrol cars—all with lights flashing—were parked in the immediate area. "Naked man," however, was not the least bit interested in all the attention he had attracted on the ground below. He was in the midst of dealing with his Maker and his stuff.

In the meantime, it looked like a couple of young patrol officers were getting ready to climb up to the roof. We did not know each other very well, and not caring to insert myself, I kind of hung back. Then again, I thought that I'd better let these guys know what they might be up against here.

After a few minutes, I took the initiative to walk up to the officers and give them a little warning. "Just to let you know," I offered, "if you go hands-on with this guy, it'd be good to go full force and get him into custody quickly."

The officers kind of stared at me with a "yeah, whatever" look. So I backed off and thought, *Okay, let's see how this goes.*

Within the next few minutes, the officers climbed to the top of that roof, and as "naked man" lowered one of his arms, I saw one of the officers reach for "naked man's" wrist (just as the officer had been trained to do) and attempt to put that wrist behind "naked man's" own back.

However, "naked man" would have none of it. All at once, he came unhinged. His important conversation with God had been interrupted and the fight was on.

Arms and legs were flying, and there was naked…naked…naked… everywhere. Fortunately, each Lubbock police officer carries a taser, and the officer applied it. And I remember thinking, *that taser's having very little effect on him.*

Eventually, the cops were able to subdue "naked man" enough to belt him into a plastic gurney. But it wasn't over. All at once, "naked man" broke the belt on that plastic gurney, and again, there was naked, naked, naked…and taser, taser, taser.

Soon, up came a sturdier backboard with more belts, and this time, "naked man" was not strong enough.

Afterwards, when it was all over and the officers had finally made their way back down, I noticed that they seemed to be breathing a little more heavily.

I was tempted to ask, *So…how did that go for you guys?* But I refrained.

That call ended okay for everyone involved, and will always be another humorous story to tell. But the important fact to remember is that when a person is running around in public, naked, he is usually doing so due to one of two reasons: he is hopped up on some type of drug, or he is hopped up from a mental condition and is often capable of extreme strength. In both scenarios, this person can be very unpredictable and very dangerous, more dangerous than many people, even new officers, appreciate.

Speaking of dangerous, naked men, let's return to the incident of November 21, 2003. (Please note that in the following story, all civilian names have been changed.)

The Negotiation

At 5:02 a.m., the police received a report of a civil disturbance in an apartment on the south side of town. The caller stated to Dispatch that a *naked man* with a 9mm semiautomatic handgun was in the apartment threatening to rape his girlfriend.

Within minutes, Sergeant Ross Hester and two officers arrived at the scene and spoke with the caller, Michael Suders, age 26. Michael stated that his girlfriend, Tammy Lytle, age 23 (whom he had known for approximately three years), was being held hostage by her ex-boyfriend, Adam Cline, age 24.

Michael told the officers that he and Tammy were in bed when Adam entered the apartment with a gun and ordered Michael to leave. Michael then fled to a neighbor's house to call 911. At this point, he wasn't sure if Adam was still in the apartment with Tammy or not.

With this brief information, the officers approached the front door to the apartment and found it standing open. They audibly identified themselves, yelling, "Police!" but they received no response.

They cautiously continued moving into the front room, a living room, but did not locate anyone. They did, however, observe that the back door to the same room was also standing open. They then moved into the adjoining kitchen, which was next to the bedroom.

65th Dr.

As they advanced a few steps, one of the officers called out, "Tammy!?" and immediately, Tammy yelled back that Adam was holding her at gunpoint in the bedroom. She pleaded with the officers to leave, and she screamed, "He's got a f---ing gun to my head. Get the f--- out!"

At the same time, Adam spoke up and calmly declared, "You guys need to move away from the kitchen, or it's gonna be bad." Adam wouldn't say what he was going to do; he just simply said that it would "be bad."

Sergeant Hester (the patrol supervisor who also happened to be a negotiator) then left the apartment to notify the shift commander of a barricaded gunman holding a hostage, while the other two officers maintained control of the living room. At the same time, other arriving officers began to evacuate the surrounding apartments. Within a few minutes, Sergeant Hester returned to the apartment.

Meanwhile, Michael provided more background to one of the responding officers. His information included the following: Michael and his girlfriend, Tammy, had arrived at the apartment about 3:45 a.m. and were already in bed when Adam entered and walked into the bedroom. Adam was holding a 9mm handgun.

Adam started to take off his shirt and told Michael to go into the bathroom (which could only be accessed through the bedroom). As Michael was following Adam's orders, he heard Adam begin to yell obscenities at Tammy. Adam's focus was on her…and not on Michael.

Michael then heard Adam begin to unzip his pants, and so he pleaded with Adam to leave Tammy alone. In response, Adam told Michael to close the bathroom door, which Michael refused to do. When Michael looked out from the bathroom into the bedroom, he saw Adam totally nude and on top of Tammy in the bed. Michael then hurriedly asked Adam if he could have his own clothing, and Adam threw Michael a shirt.

Michael then asked Adam for his gun. At first, Adam wouldn't relinquish it. Eventually, though, Michael was able to convince Adam to give him the magazine from the gun. Michael quickly ejected the chambered round, then placed the round and the magazine on the bathroom counter. Adam, however, maintained possession of the gun.

The Negotiation

Next, Adam grabbed Tammy by the hair, and while he was dragging Tammy towards the living room, he demanded that Michael walk in front of them (the magazine and ammunition were left lying on the bathroom counter).

At that point, Tammy started to struggle, and Michael believed that she had knocked the gun free. At that point, Michael lunged toward Adam. Adam, however, regained possession of the gun and pointed it at Michael. Adam then told Michael to leave the apartment, and while Michael was running out the back door, he saw that Adam was pulling Tammy back into the bedroom. According to Michael, he then rushed to a neighbor's apartment to call the police. Michael also mentioned that Tammy had been worried about how violent and controlling Adam had become since their breakup.

The SWAT callout was initiated at 5:30 a.m. Accordingly, the SWAT team, negotiators, and neighborhood services arrived (they come with the command RV, support gear, and other necessary equipment). The command post was set up approximately one and one-half blocks away from Tammy's apartment.

I was also paged, as a member of the negotiating team. This would be my first official, full-scale callout, and this time I had some training and experience.

When I arrived at the command post, I went to the back of the RV to meet with the SWAT commander and other police negotiators, and to receive a verbal update about the situation. Throughout the day, we would continue to meet and talk with one another. To ensure more convenient and swift communication, our negotiating team also made use of a marker board on which all police and negotiation staff could quickly read and write pertinent and new information—details about the hostage's residence, characteristics of the bad guy and his demands, personal information provided by family members, and any other important data.

Police were informed that Adam had graduated from nearby Roosevelt High School in 1997 and subsequently served in the US Marines from 1997 to 2001. At some time during his service, he was a Military

Policeman on the Special Reaction Team. We were also told that he had been injured when shot in the foot by friendly fire.

In addition, at some point early on in this incident, Adam stated that he had recently graduated from South Plains College Fire Fighting Academy and EMT school. He claimed that he was not afraid of anything. He knew SWAT would be on their way and he was waiting for them. He insisted that the end result of the situation would be determined by the police.

As I listened to the details of Michael's statement and learned a little of Adam's personal history as well as his communication with the police thus far, I felt strongly that we were possibly dealing with a psychopath, and this would be a very difficult and dangerous situation.

In my training and work as a counselor, I've become aware of the common characteristics of a psychopath. This person usually doesn't have the ability to establish meaningful relational attachments because of excessive selfishness. He (though women can also be psychopaths, it's just less common) is often confident, even arrogant, and believes other points of view are unnecessary. He feels that no one else can do something as well as he can. He doesn't feel that he ever fails; therefore, he is incapable of learning from experience or from his own mistakes. He will keep repeating the same behavior. (Therapists call this a lack of insight because this person doesn't realize the implications of their behavior.) If something does turn out badly, he refuses to accept blame. Rather, it is someone else's fault. He may have trouble tolerating certain types of stress, but is seemingly unfazed by other stressors. He is a bold person. He exhibits little fear. A dangerous situation doesn't bother him. He has no problem defying authority and even gets excited about it. In many cases he doesn't care if his actions are considered illegal. He is impulsive and does whatever he wants to do, regardless of whom his actions may hurt and regardless of what anyone else thinks. He exhibits little self-control or restraint. If he wants something, he simply takes it. Many people say he lacks a conscience. He can easily commit violent acts and feel no guilt, remorse, or empathy for his victims. He can be a cruel and cold-hearted person, have no desire to help others, or feel sorry for anyone. Rather, he uses his power to exploit and manipulate. He doesn't think like a "normal" person. He is wired differently, especially when it comes to emotions. Unfortunately, treatment for this condition is, at best, complicated and takes a very long time.

Also alarming is the fact that a psychopath cannot always be easily spotted. He often appears to be normal and can be endearing, turning the charm on and off like a switch.

Now, let's consider Adam and what I had already learned about him early on the morning of November 21, 2003.

His appearance: he was naked, which as I said before, usually means a person is hopped up on something or hopped up from a mental condition.

His focus: Adam wanted Tammy and wanted her to pay attention to him. But Tammy's focus was on Michael. So, Adam "eliminated" Michael by telling him to go into the bathroom, then told him to close the bathroom door, and eventually ordered him to leave the apartment. Tammy's family later mentioned that Adam killed (eliminated) her dog when he felt she was paying too much attention to it.

His conversation and attitude: Adam claimed he wasn't afraid of anything. (Remember, a psychopath has little or no fear.) He also stated the end result would be determined by the police, suggesting he wouldn't be responsible for anything bad that happened. Rather, it would be the fault of police. His instructions to the police, that they move away from the kitchen "or it's gonna be bad," indicated he was determined to be in control. His use of vague communication already revealed that he liked to manipulate and would play games to keep us wondering and guessing throughout the day. His vague language also indicated he knew not to make direct threats because then the police would have to respond.

His actions and behavior: He was bold. He had broken into a home that was not his. This was a dangerous situation, yet he didn't seem to be bothered by it. He was already standing up to the police and their authority, saying that he knew SWAT was coming and he "was waiting for them." In addition, having experience as a Military Policeman on a

Special Reaction Team with the Marines, he was aware of SWAT tactics and negotiation skills, and by his language, he was confident that he was good at it. If I was right about him being a psychopath, I knew it would be extremely difficult to talk with him, especially because he would not be capable of building a rapport or establishing a relationship with anyone. In addition, he wouldn't be capable of receiving or showing empathy. So, essentially, we could throw everything out that we had learned in basic negotiator school.

Finally, just as a psychopath is often violent, Adam had also committed several violent acts. He was currently holding a woman at gunpoint. He had been screaming obscenities at Tammy and pulling her around the apartment by her hair. And then we learned of his other recent violence and repeated abnormal behavior.

A month earlier, sometime in October 2003, Adam had been arrested when a motorist noticed him pulling Tammy's hair as the two were traveling in a vehicle. Subsequently, however, an assault charge was dropped against Adam in favor of a lesser charge.

Then, on October 17, 2003, a neighbor called police to report a suspicious man with a backpack outside Tammy's apartment.

Three days later, on October 20, 2003, Adam broke into Tammy's apartment and chased her and her sister with a knife. He left behind a backpack containing two knives, duct tape, handcuffs, gloves, a flashlight, and a camcorder. Subsequently, he was arrested on a charge of burglary with intent to commit a felony. In Texas, this was throwing the book at him. According to testimony, both women claimed that they feared for their lives. Adam was indicted by a grand jury. However, he was allowed to post bail on the condition that he would not contact Tammy.

Adam was then released on Friday, October 31, 2003, and Tammy obtained a protective order against him on November 6. We also heard that when she selected her current apartment, she did so specifically because it had deadbolts on the doors and a bedroom without doors, windows, or access from the outside.

Now, 23 days after Adam had been released, he was holding Tammy hostage in this same bedroom and had barricaded the bedroom

The Negotiation

door with a bunch of furniture. What Tammy was hoping would keep her safe—limited access to the bedroom—was now enabling Adam to hold her hostage and, at the same time, causing problems for the police.

The callout had been initiated at 5:30 a.m., and when extra officers arrived at the apartment, negotiators Sergeant Ross Hester and Corporal Sharon Casey relocated to the command post.

At approximately 6:25 a.m., Sergeant Caspell then attempted to make verbal contact with Adam and Tammy by telephone. These attempts, however, were unsuccessful.

Soon, a SWAT member within the apartment notified Command that due to Adam's elevated emotional state, they needed a negotiator on the premises. Sergeant Hester and Corporal Casey, trained police negotiators, were then sent back to the apartment to talk with Adam, while other officers continued to attempt telephone communication. Hester and Casey set up positions inside the living room along a brick wall and would be talking from the living room, through the kitchen, towards the bedroom door.

Corporal Casey, as primary negotiator, immediately began to call out to Adam and Tammy. Right away, however, Adam became very agitated. He refused to speak to a woman and yelled out, "I'm gonna kill her if that woman doesn't shut up." Adam agreed, however, to continue to talk with Sergeant Ross Hester. Consequently, roles were switched at 6:38 a.m.

Corporal Casey assumed the role as secondary negotiator and was responsible for relaying progress reports to us back in the command vehicle (like an RV) via phone and radio, outside of Adam's earshot. The telephone attempts from the command vehicle to contact Adam were then abandoned.

Sergeant Hester started conversations with Adam, trying to calm him down while at the same time asking a few questions. Adam would not talk for very long and would cut off most conversations with vague statements such as, "I'll get back with you," or "I'm thinkin' about it," or "In a little while."

At times, negotiators had trouble hearing Adam due to the fact that they were trying to carry on conversations across the living room, through the kitchen and hallway, as well as through a closed, barricaded bedroom door. Then, the oven timer started to go off every three to five minutes, causing even more hearing difficulty and impeding conversation. Sergeant Hester was able to get Adam to concede that the timer should be turned off so that everyone could be heard.

Subsequently, SWAT discovered that they could control the timer through an external breaker and decided to use it to their advantage. They would turn the timer off, but then turn it back on again whenever they needed to cover up the sound of moving their equipment and personnel.

During the next hour, Sergeant Hester also tried to talk with Adam about the military and attempted to find some other hooks, but nothing seemed to work in developing any rapport. Adam continued to give noncommittal answers.

After about two hours of this, I grabbed a sheet of notebook paper and jotted down a few negotiation suggestions. This list was then hand-carried and delivered by a SWAT officer from the command post to the apartment and given to Sergeant Hester.

Along with the suggested negotiation strategies, I also decided to add some humorous comments in an effort to boost morale. Ross had been up all night, the standoff had been going on for a few hours, and this was a difficult conversation in a tense situation. Consequently, I figured he could use some encouragement. And so, at the bottom of the note, I wrote a comment or two to lighten his mood, emphasizing my "everlasting" support from a distance. Then I signed the note, "Love, Andy."

Due to my inexperience, I didn't realize that everything within the premises of the apartment would eventually become evidence, including my little "love note." Fortunately, no harm was done. When I later viewed pictures taken by the crime scene photographer, I noticed that the bottom of my note had been folded under and taped to a box of donuts sitting on a fish tank (yep! donuts). I could read only the top portion of my list that began with: "What keeps you from coming out?

What is the worst part of this for you? What do you think is the worst thing that …?" Fortunately, the CSI guy covered for me, and I'm now grateful that my love note is not a matter of public record.

I'm not sure if my list of suggestions contributed to any part of Sergeant Hester's conversations, but by 7:15 a.m., Adam had calmed down and was now talking.

At 7:42 a.m., it seemed some rapport was established during conversations about high school days at Roosevelt High. During this discussion, Adam began to cry. At 8:00 a.m., he was still crying but calm. At 9:00 a.m., Sergeant Hester suggested, "Hey, how about we end all this and you come out in five minutes?" Adam ignored the semi-deadline, and nothing happened. (No harm in trying.) At 9:30 a.m., Adam was calm, but not ready to exit. At 10:00 a.m., there was no change. At 10:05 a.m., Tammy called out that she was all right.

At this point, right around 10:00 a.m., Sergeant Jon Caspell (another police negotiator on the team) and I left the RV and were standing outside. He asked, "Andy, what do you think? How do you think this is gonna go? Murder-suicide?"

I replied, "I think he is going to kill her. Then he'll try to kill a bunch of us. Then he's probably going to kill himself."

He nodded and said, "Okay."

We'd been on scene for about five hours and we were no closer to peaceful resolution, nor had there been much change in Adam's course of action or response to all of Ross's efforts.

At noon, Corporal Casey notified command that Sergeant Ross Hester was showing signs of fatigue. Ross had worked the third shift the night before, and had been on this callout since 5:00 a.m.

I learned in training that it's not ideal to change a primary negotiator once he or she has established some type of rapport with the subject. In this case, Ross had now spent approximately seven hours trying to develop a relationship with Adam and hopefully had gained some of his trust. Starting over with someone else was not appealing, and Ross didn't want to leave. Yet he realized his own limitations. Moreover, we had no idea how much longer this standoff would last.

It was soon decided by command staff that Sergeant Jon Caspell would take over, and so began the process of changing negotiators.

At 12:30 p.m., Sergeant Caspell entered the apartment to relieve Sergeant Hester. Sergeant Hester then introduced Sergeant Caspell and began to prepare Adam for the switch, explaining that he, as a negotiator, needed to take a break and get some rest. Not surprisingly, Adam didn't like it and insisted that he would not talk to anyone but Hester. Adam made statements such as, "You can't do that. I don't want this." (In hindsight, this seemed to be a classic psychopathic power play.) Consequently, to help keep Adam calm, Sergeant Hester continued to negotiate for a short while longer and then transitioned Sergeant Caspell into the role of primary negotiator.

Ross and I took a long walk around the neighborhood afterwards in an effort to decompress. The stress of being a primary negotiator is difficult to appreciate until you are in the hot seat, yourself. I remember working a patrol shift one night and hearing over the radio that someone was poised to jump off an overpass from the highway that circles the city (Loop 289). I arrived to find a patrol officer, John Hayes, speaking with a man sitting on the guardrail. If memory serves, we were up there talking with this man about his family and work troubles for about an hour. John did a great job talking to this man, and eventually the man decided to come down and go to the ambulance we had waiting for him on the overpass (I'll come back to this story in more detail in chapter 5). Once the man was safely in custody, John turned to me and said something like, "Man, that is like running a mental marathon!" He was gassed. Ross was weary too. He'd been up since yesterday evening, and his adrenaline had been pumping while talking with Adam for that last seven hours or so.

At 12:52 p.m., Sergeant Caspell officially took over as primary negotiator and did a great job of reassuring Adam that he would do everything he could to work with him and resolve this situation peacefully.

When we switched negotiators, we most likely should have lost something in the way of rapport with Adam. But it was soon apparent that we didn't lose any trust or relationship. Instead, he seemed to settle down quickly with the new negotiator. The switch seemed to go well, which on the one hand was good; on the other hand, it indicated that we hadn't really accomplished anything. Again, I thought of a psychopath and the inability to establish a relationship. I continued to worry that this was going to end badly no matter what we did.

At 1:00 p.m., Corporal Mora replaced Corporal Casey as secondary negotiator, and it was also around this time that I discussed the outcome of this situation with one of the SWAT lieutenants and a sergeant. When they asked what I thought would happen, I repeated what Jon and I discussed earlier, "I think he is going to kill her, he's going to try and kill a bunch of us, then he'll kill himself."

Meanwhile, Caspell continued to assure Adam that he would work with him to resolve the situation. By 1:30 p.m., Adam sounded calm and even-toned.

For the next few hours, Sergeant Caspell would continually ask Adam to come out peacefully. Adam's answer was, again, always something along the lines of "I'm thinking about it." He continued to be very vague, but non-threatening. He made no demands and didn't ask for anything. He wouldn't negotiate. This situation did not fit the definition of "negotiable." At times, Adam could be heard talking calmly to Tammy and occasionally laughing. Seems everything was just as Adam wanted it to be.

Throughout the afternoon hours, I also performed my role as a victim services counselor and met with Tammy's mother and some other relatives. I tried to give them as much information as I could, reassure them of our efforts, provide support, and attempt to help them process their thoughts and emotions.

At about 2:00 p.m., intelligence developed about a possible third-party intermediary (TPI). A close friend of Adam's had shown up at the command post and believed that Adam would talk to him.

Some other negotiators and I spent some time talking to this friend, finding out if he was stable, if he could handle the stress, and if he could act responsibly. Likewise, we needed to know if he would respond well to our suggestions and listen to our coaching—in order to get some idea of how it would go if we allowed him to talk to Adam on our behalf. I knew that TPIs should be used only as a last resort. However, at this point, over seven hours into the standoff and seemingly not getting anywhere with Adam, we were willing to consider this option.

Once we had a sense of this guy, we decided we would give it a try if and when the situation was right.

When we were ready, Sergeant Caspell made an offer to Adam. "If you send out Tammy, if you'll let Tammy go, we'll let you talk to your friend who is here."

It didn't fly.

Adam flatly rejected the offer and adamantly refused to allow Tammy to leave the bedroom. At the same time, Tammy attempted to say something to the officers through the door. But as soon as she began to talk, two slaps could be heard, and she immediately stopped talking. Then, all of a sudden, she began speaking again.

When I heard of this situation, I wondered why this had happened. Why didn't Adam want her to say whatever she was about to say? Why did he then slap her? And why then did she start talking almost immediately again? Perhaps he knew that she had better start talking as quickly as possible to give us the impression that she was doing just fine. He was well aware that if the authorities felt she was in imminent danger, they would come in, and maybe he wasn't ready for that just yet.

Adam then mentioned that a dog was with them in the bedroom, and he was willing to exchange the dog for a pack of cigarettes and a lighter. In negotiator school, I learned that in many cases, small trades eventually lead to larger ones. And so, Adam's offer gave us hope. This was his first demand and a good sign.

The chief of police insisted that we would provide only one lit cigarette, not a pack, and definitely not a lighter. The SWAT team would need to deliver the cigarette with a shield in front of them in exchange for the dog. And we all began to orchestrate the trade.

Soon, Adam was un-barricading the door, which took him from three to five minutes. He then had Tammy reach out for the cigarette, and at 2:50 p.m., the exchange was complete.

The Negotiation

Through this action, we knew how much of a barricade Adam had created. Officers also discussed getting some type of fiber optics under the door so they could see what was going on in that room, but the barricade was blocking any access.

I was glad we retrieved the dog and hoped for more. But when I informed Tammy's family of the outcome, they became extremely upset, insisting that Adam loved that dog and would be less likely to hurt Tammy if the dog had remained in the room. I was surprised by this information.

After this exchange, Adam was asked again if he would be willing to talk to his friend. But he refused, so this idea was abandoned altogether. It seemed this friend meant nothing to Adam.

Communications then stalled. So Sergeant Caspell brought up an earlier conversation that Sergeant Hester had with Adam in which Adam stated that he, himself, would come out as a "winner" if he decided to come out with his hands up. Adam was then asked to give a time frame, but he refused. In response to some of Caspell's other requests, Adam again replied, "I'm thinking about it."

Then, Adam and Tammy could be heard talking to each other. Voices were faint; exact words could not be deciphered; but the tone sounded upbeat.

At 4:30 p.m., specific conversation could be heard between Adam and Tammy as they reminisced about family and friends for approximately one hour. They sounded like they were laughing at their recollections. Perhaps Tammy was doing whatever she could in order to save her life.

When Sergeant Caspell heard their conversation, he attempted to also talk with Adam about family and friends, but it didn't get us anywhere. Adam continued to refuse to release Tammy or negotiate an end to this standoff.

At 5:30 p.m., Corporal Melugin relieved Corporal Mora as secondary negotiator. Also during this time, an attempt was made to talk to Adam about fatigue, hunger, and concern for their physical welfare. Adam remarked that they were fine. Offers of food and water were quickly dismissed.

Negotiations bogged down again, but there was no indication that immediate SWAT action was needed. We'd been at this now for 12 hours and had expended a lot of mental and emotional energy. At 6:00 p.m., when the negotiators again made an attempt to talk about Adam and Tammy coming out, all efforts were resisted. Adam simply said, "I'll think about it" and "I need more time to talk with Tammy." When asked if he would hurt Tammy, Adam assured the officers that he would not.

At 6:30 pm, our Emergency Rescue Vehicle (ERV) was staged outside the west wall of the apartment. At this point, I thought that we should change tactics with this guy and suggested, "Let's not settle with 'I'm thinking about it. I need more time.' Let's use a different approach. Let's tell him that his answers are not acceptable any longer. Let's press him for hard and fast answers and see how it goes."

At 7:00 p.m., Sergeant Caspell changed his approach. Adam was informed that command was requiring "hard and fast answers" and that noncommittal answers would no longer suffice. Sergeant Caspell reinforced the guarantee that he was there to work *with* Adam, but needed input from him on how to end the incident peacefully.

Again Adam gave a noncommittal answer, still saying, "I'm thinking about it."

This time, his statement was rejected by Sergeant Caspell. "No, Adam, that's not going to work."

Adam said, "Okay. Give me 60 minutes and I'll come out."

That response surprised us all.

Sergeant Caspell agreed to Adam's suggestion, and every ten minutes during the next hour, he would continually remind Adam of the deal that they had made and notify him of the amount of time left before surrender.

A few times, Sergeant Caspell would also review with Adam the exit strategy. "Un-barricade the door…come out without a weapon… let us see your hands…comply with commands," knowing that Adam was still armed and dangerous.

At 7:50 p.m., Sergeant Caspell stated, "You've got 10 minutes left, Adam. Why don't you start un-barricading the door?"

Adam pushed back with a typical psychopathic power play and said, "No, I'll start un-barricading after I get my full 60 minutes."

Ten minutes later, at 8:00 p.m., Sergeant Caspell called out, "You've had your 60 minutes, Adam."

Adam then replied, "I'm working on un-barricading the door."

However, no sounds were heard to support that claim.

Sergeant Caspell and Adam continued to converse about removing the barricade, and at one point, Adam said, "I'm gonna have Tammy help me remove the barricade."

Sergeant Caspell reminded Adam, "You gave me your word that you would come out."

Finally, Sergeant Caspell and SWAT began to hear what sounded like furniture being moved.

At this time, I was standing next to Lieutenant Roger Ellis in the command post. We were viewing a TV screen located at the front of the RV, which provided a closed-circuit feed from a camera pointed at the front door of the apartment. Soon, someone called over the radio, "Suspect is un-barricading the door. Looks like they're coming out."

The chief was standing in front of us and raised his hands in celebration. Although our hopes were extremely high, I turned to Lieutenant Ellis and said, "They're not out yet."

Sergeant Caspell then began to thank Adam for following through on his promise, when all of a sudden, while Caspell was in mid-sentence, we heard several gunshots, fired in rapid succession inside the bedroom.

Immediately, SWAT initiated a tactical response, and negotiators vacated the building. Distraction devices were deployed, and the breaching team inside charged down the hallway to the bedroom door. Suddenly, another round of shots were heard, and the lead rescue team member fell backwards as he swung a ram at the door again. A tactical medic then grabbed him from behind and dragged him out of the way by his helmet. Later, they discovered that the officer who had fallen wasn't hit by a bullet but had simply lost his footing just as the rounds started flying.

Fortunately for the officers inside, when Adam was shooting through the closed bedroom door towards them, he wasn't squared up to the door, which meant that he was shooting at an angle into the kitchen instead of straight out the door into the hallway. Consequently, most of the shots missed the officers.

Meanwhile, as expected, they encountered problems getting into the room because Adam had not un-barricaded the bedroom door, and the obstructions were preventing them from accessing the room.

At the same time, a flash-bang device was used by SWAT to create a diversion, and the ERV with a battering ram was utilized to break through the west brick wall, directly outside of Tammy's bedroom.

The first SWAT officer to enter the bedroom through the outside hole was one of our guys who goes away for long periods of time to serve with a Special Forces unit in the Army—and that's about all we knew of his military job. That's the kind of guy you want to go first through the door, and he was the first to find Adam lying on his back on the bed.

Adam was moving and armed with a pistol. The officers, however, were able to immediately secure the pistol. But when they attempted to handcuff Adam, he struggled and resisted. Eventually, the officers turned Adam over, and at that point, they discovered that he had sustained three, self-inflicted, close-contact gunshot wounds in his left upper chest, which indicated that the 9mm semiautomatic Beretta had been pushed up against his body.

Tammy was located on the bathroom floor, lying in a pool of blood. She had been shot eight times.

Directly, she was transported by ambulance to University Medical Center in Lubbock, but died in the emergency room.

Adam, likewise, was taken to University Medical Center. He would die during surgery at approximately 9:45 p.m.

Later that night, detectives documented 17 spent shell casings in the bedroom. Six shots had been fired towards officers in the kitchen. An officer and a tactical medic had been hit but not injured. One officer found a bullet hole through his right upper-arm sleeve; somehow, the bullet had missed his arm completely. Another officer found a bullet lodged in the cord of his police radio after having glanced off the collar of his vest. It was just resting there in his mic cord. Silly physics.

During the entire rescue, police did not fire any shots.

On November 24, 2003, the *Lubbock Avalanche-Journal* published the obituaries for Tammy Lytle and Adam Cline. They appeared on the same page just inches from each other.

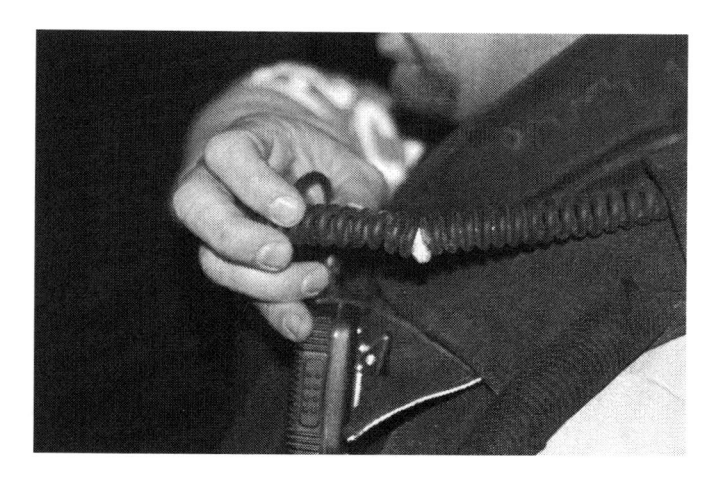

* * *

The entire Lubbock Police Department was heavy-hearted at the horrific outcome. Even now, several years later, this 15-hour standoff is still very frustrating and a tough one to handle. While most hostage/negotiation incidents end peacefully, this situation, most regrettably, did not.

Throughout that fateful day, the police determined that a forced entry at any time would have immediately escalated the situation and endangered Tammy. All the while, they remained hopeful that the incident would end with a smooth and tranquil resolution. Our goal was to get Tammy out alive, and from my point of view, we did everything we could to accomplish that task, especially since we did not have access to explosive breaching. That was due, in part, to the long-term effects of what happened in 2001 on the callout that killed Sergeant Cox. The SWAT officers licensed to conduct explosive breaching were no longer on the team. Looking back, however, I realize we never were able to truly negotiate with Adam. Sgt. Hester and Sgt. Caspell did everything they could to talk to Adam, but he would have none of it. This, coupled with the inability to get to Tammy and move her to safety before Adam could act, led to a stalemate—with Adam in control.

My sympathy and condolences continue to be extended to Tammy's family and friends, as well as to Adam's.

CHAPTER FOUR
RISING TO THE CHALLENGE

Sitting down at my desk, I made my way through stack after stack of police records. My goal was to check off every call I'd responded to, and suddenly, I grew very tired. Shuffling through the first 10 years of my work, I'd counted 56 suicides, 33 attempted suicides, 18 homicides (sometimes with multiple victims), 22 sexual assaults, 50 "natural" deaths, 22 "natural" infant or child deaths, 16 traffic accidents (1 fatality, 15 with serious injuries), 96 domestic disputes of varying severity, 12 death notifications, 7 SWAT callouts, 4 officer-involved lethal force incidents, 6 in-the-line-of-duty officer deaths (not all at LPD), and countless aggravated assaults, stabbings, robberies, and burglaries.

Why was I doing this? I knew better. In my line of work as a MHP and an educator in psychology and counseling, I knew these morbid stories of sorrow should not be digested in just one bite; rather, I should be dealing with just *one* call, *one* person, *one* family…*one* moment at a time. That's what I often told each stranger I had met, "Let's deal with 'right now,' and help you get through the next hour." This job has never had a schedule but I've always been conscious of the purpose: to bring a little light in those first dark moments, a little peace, and even the hope of healing to those who've been assailed by some unforeseeable ordeal—to be an umbrella in the midst of a storm.

But what happens after the ambulance crew and the firefighters leave, when the detectives have finished asking their questions and the medical examiner is done taking his pictures, after all the strobe lights have been turned off and the officers head to their next call?

A crisis counselor, like me, and other members of our crisis team remain to comfort the family and manage any number of "little things" for those returning to a house that has been forever changed. We stay and do the best we can, attempting to help each person transition back from the surreal to what is now a new life—except, there's nothing really new about a hollow room emptied of happiness and joy; but the place where the smell, the blood, and the vomit remain. Where all at once, shock turns into horror, and a tear-streaked face turns to me with that haunting question, "What do I do now?"

It's not easy to encounter these grim and disheartening situations. Yet our Crisis Team members continue to get up in the middle of the night and rush off to another crisis scene because our presence seems to make a difference in peoples' lives in the most difficult of times.

I'll come back to stories about this line of work in chapter 5. For some, it might be interesting to hear about the details of our Crisis Team program and some statistics about our work, officer and victim perceptions of the team, and about the people on the team. If reading about statistics makes you homicidal, then I suggest you skip ahead to chapter 5.

From 2003 to 2008, our Victim Services Crisis Team at the Lubbock Police Department grew from seven volunteers to about 20. At that time, I, along with a colleague, Jill Fuller, and a student, Briana Riley, researched the joint work effort between the MHPs and the officers of the Lubbock Police Department and subsequently co-wrote the article, "On-scene Mental Health Counseling Provided Through Police Departments," published in the *Journal of Mental Health Counseling* (October 2008).[2]

---

2 For complete information, please see: Andy T. Young, Jill Fuller, Briana Riley, "On-scene Mental Health Counseling Provided Through Police Departments," *Journal of Mental Health Counseling*, Volume 30, Number 4 (American Mental Health Counselors As-

One main purpose of our Crisis Team was to help people emotionally process a traumatic event and ease the acute symptoms suffered as the result of a crisis. This help is most effective when it occurs immediately after the crisis, instead of several days to weeks later. Likewise, in our personal experience, we realized that some sort of psychological intervention provided quickly after a trauma was extremely beneficial, as it met the immediate and practical needs of victims. Some people call this psychological first aid (PFA), which includes such assistance as engaging a victim in conversation, helping to keep that person calm, providing safety, gathering information, addressing concerns, offering suggestions on how to cope, and distributing information regarding the legal and investigative systems, as well as information about social support and other helpful organizations.

Once our police department in Lubbock established a Crisis Team, I learned that there were other police departments that did not have specific personnel or a special program to deal with victims such as the mentally ill or those involved in domestic-related disputes. Or if they did, the programs fell into one of three categories: First, the police officers had been trained to respond to these types of calls and serve as a liaison with mental health services. Second, police officers contacted MHP consultants and they provided their services together. Third, a mental health team was established within a law enforcement agency (otherwise called a Crisis Team) that responded to the scene (this model is the rarest of the three). This is the type the Lubbock Police Department chose to put into operation in order to reduce the amount of time officers spent dealing with domestic calls, and at the same time freeing officers to perform duties for which they were better trained. Our department successfully uses this type of crisis intervention program to this day.

---

sociation, Alexandria, VA: October 2008), pp. 345-361. (Please also see the article entitled, "On-scene Mental Health Services: A Case Study of the Lubbock Police Department's Victims Services Crisis Team," published in the September 2009 issue of the *FBI Law Enforcement Bulletin*, US Department of Justice, Federal Bureau of Investigation, pp. 6-11, written by Andrew T. Young, Ed. D., L.P.C. and Neal Brumley, M.S.)

Not long after our Crisis Team went to work, we soon discovered MHPs could be used in many other capacities in addition to domestic violence situations. Consequently, during the next several years, our team grew and helped stabilize a myriad of volatile situations, as well as assist with all types of victims.

In addition to providing the information above to the *Journal of Mental Health Counseling*, my coauthors and I also determined to familiarize other departments and communities with the benefits of our on-scene, crisis-counseling unit.

Accordingly, we sought to provide answers to the following questions:

1. In what types of situations was the Crisis Team used and what types of help were provided?
2. What did the Lubbock police officers think about our Crisis Team?
3. What did the victims think about our Crisis Team?
4. Who served as volunteers on our Crisis Team?

I'd like to share some of the findings we discovered as a result of this research. While statistics are something that make me all warm and fuzzy, I've elected to forgo charts and graphs and instead, simply list some short quotes and interesting facts from this article that readily reveal the effectiveness of our Crisis Team, and likewise, support the importance of establishing such help in every community.

In What Types of Situations Was the Crisis Team Used and What Types of Help Were Provided?

From 2000 to 2007, our Crisis Team responded to hundreds of situations in which police officers requested Crisis Team involvement by paging the MHP coordinator throughout the week, who then assembled volunteers to respond. Moreover, when volunteers reported to work on a Friday or Saturday night shift, the team of two had access to an in-car computer that provided information regarding every call to which officers were responding, and to which the team could self-initiate a response if it could be determined that the scene was safe and the situation might benefit from the presence of a mental health professional.

In addition to domestic disturbances and domestic violence calls, these crisis situations included completed suicides, attempted suicides, suicidal ideation, murders, death investigations, child death traffic accidents/traffic fatalities, sexual assault calls, child/elderly abuse, mental illness, burglaries/robberies/shoplifting, missing persons, kidnappings, runaways, nondomestic assault, chemically dependent subjects, and assisting officers involved in lethal force incidents.

Our team also assisted in less frequent calls such as helping a homeless family after a house fire, finding child care after service of a drug warrant, and deaths that occurred from a boating accident and at a construction site.

Our most typical action performed was crisis counseling, which involved multiple tasks, many of them performed simultaneously. Rising to the challenge in moments of chaos and confusion, our team members, while providing a calming presence, often had to immediately assess if any people at the scene of crisis were a danger to themselves, and if so, coordinate/consult with officers to initiate an emergency or medical response. At times, volunteers were also required to assess all at-risk individuals (children, the elderly, and the disabled) to assure safety and support and to contact agencies as required by law. Providing temporary child care was involved sometimes as well. Our Crisis Team members were there to help victims grieve, emotionally and mentally process the devastating experience, guide them through reality and set immediate goals, and offer an opportunity to ventilate feelings and discuss the events that occurred. At times, we explained victim's rights and victim's compensation; provided information on what type of symptoms victims might suffer; developed a plan on how to deal with the crisis in the next hours and days; and explained the investigative, judicial and/or medical systems. On other occasions, our team assisted in contacting sources of social and legal support, protected victims from the media, and helped petition for an Emergency Protective Order (EPO). Additionally, we would act as liaison between victims and law enforcement officers, coordinate with both parties, pass along information, and give statements to detectives; other times, we provided transportation for the victim and family members.[3]

Team members were likewise mindful of the difficulties victims would face when everyone had left the scene. Consequently, we would offer to help individuals with such tasks as retrieving items from a residence during a death investigation, packing a suitcase, and discarding any items that were damaged as a result of the crisis.

What Did Lubbock Police Officers Think About the Crisis Team?

I asked officers to provide information that would reveal how often and in what capacity they used the Crisis Team, what they thought about a Crisis Team, and how helpful the Crisis Team was to the police department. Participation in the survey was voluntary. Appropriate forms were distributed on December 1, 2005 and then gathered by January 9, 2006. Officers of all ranks participated—patrolmen, corporals, sergeants, lieutenants, and captains. Specifically, we asked:

"When the Crisis Team responded, I would characterize them as...."

There were approximately 285 officers, supervisors, and commanders in the Patrol, Persons Crimes, Juvenile, and Special Operations divisions at the beginning of 2006. Of these, 91 completed the survey (a response rate of 32%), and 73 reported using the Crisis Team on at least one call. Of those 73 officers using the Crisis Team, 79% reported using the Crisis Team more than once.

---

3   Ibid, see pages 350-352.

The Patrol Division, which used the Crisis Team most often, represented 88% of the sample. Detectives from the Person Crimes section comprised 10% of the sample, and the remaining 2% came from officers who did not report their division.[4]

Officers involved in the survey represented a wide range of ages, rank, and years of law enforcement experience.

Ninety-three percent of officers stated the department should keep the Crisis Team program; the other 7% left this question blank. In the space provided on the survey, responding officers stated that volunteers were able to deal directly with traumatized family members, free officers to conduct investigations, have extensive patience, have resources available for victims, are an asset that is overlooked at times, and victims are more receptive to someone not in uniform. Officers also stated volunteers should be given some type of compensation, work later hours, and work more days of the week.[5]

Law enforcement officers also had the opportunity to share their perceptions of the Crisis Team:

The officer survey also provided a checklist for ranking the helpfulness of the Crisis Team, with rankings ranging from 1 to 5. Seventy-four percent of officers (N=73) indicated that the Crisis Team was "helpful to me"; 95% indicated that the Crisis Team was "helpful to the victim(s)"; and 93% stated the Crisis Team volunteer

---

4 Ibid, page 353.
5 Ibid, page 354.

FIGHT OR FLIGHT

on their call was "courteous and professional." No negative feedback was given, though the checklist provided an opportunity to do so.

Officers (N=73) were asked to rank how well the Crisis Team fulfilled its purpose of assisting victims and officers. No officer ranked the team "poor" (1); 1% ranked it "fair" (2), 4% "adequate" (3), 41% "very well" (4), 48% "above and beyond" (5), and 6% did not answer the question...No officers ranked the team "poor" (1) or "fair" (2) when reporting the team's ability to assist officers; 14% ranked it "adequate" (3), 60% "very well' (4), 23% "above and beyond" (5), and 3% did not answer this question.[6]

We also discovered that police officers left the scene and returned to service before the Crisis Team departed on 25% of the calls, indicating that because of the team's assistance, officers were freed up to respond to other calls for service more quickly.[7]

What Did the Victims Think About Our Team?

Another part of our survey was to gather information from the people who were considered victims and who were served by the Crisis Team. We wanted to know what they thought about our program and about the volunteers who had responded to 768 calls for service.

In 2007, 190 questionnaires were mailed to victims served by the Crisis Team (2003-06) for whom addresses were accessible; of these, 97 were returned because the victim no longer lived at the address reported [many needed to relocate due to their circumstances], and 25 completed questionnaires

---

6   Ibid, page 356.
7   Ibid, see pages 352,356.

were analyzed, representing a response rate of 27% for surveys sent to correct addresses.

A death investigation was the crisis most frequently experienced by respondents (32%); three of the eight deaths were children. Seven cases were suicide (28%), three were domestic disputes (12%), two were sexual assaults (8%), and two were traffic accidents (8%). One respondent experienced an assault (4%) and one a robbery (4%). The last respondent checked the option 'other' but did not indicate what the crisis was. Nineteen respondents (76%) reported receiving a follow-up call or visit, two stated they did not receive a call or visit (8%), and four stated they could not remember (16%).[8]

Victims were asked to rank their perception of the overall helpfulness of the Crisis Team intervention at the time of the crisis and at the time of the follow-up call. On a scale from zero to ten, only one person stated the intervention was not helpful. The rest (96%) indicated a level of helpfulness from average (5) to extremely helpful (10). A mean of 8.2 indicated a level of helpfulness well above average…

The victim survey also asked respondents…to describe the Crisis Team volunteer and their helpfulness. Twenty-two respondents (88%) checked both "concerned" and "caring," 84% chose "supported my feelings," 80% indicated "supportive," 72% chose "focused," 68% marked "helped me talk about what happened," and 64% indicated both "knew what was going on" and "made the situation easier to handle." Seven other positive descriptors were each chosen once…

---

8   Ibid., pages 354-355.

Victims wrote a number of narrative responses. Examples were: "I think everything was handled in a professional manner," "They were excellent, but of course couldn't fix what was wrong," "they took very good care of my needs," "through all the sadness and grief I remember the group being so supportive, even with my son's friends," "I feel they were very helpful to me in my situation and helped me understand what was going on and were very caring to me as well as my family," and "I had someone to sit on the curb with outside of my house, otherwise I would have been alone while they were putting my dad's body in the van."[9]

According to these comments, we concluded that the team had provided meaningful assistance to victims, stabilized volatile situations, and distributed useful referral information. Volunteers were perceived as concerned, caring, and helpful.

The perceptions of helpfulness gathered through the officer and victim surveys support the conclusion that this program has value and its volunteers perform their duties well. The narrative information from victim and police officer surveys suggest the program is helpful. The results obtained through the officer survey are of particular interest. For instance, although the police culture is typically suspect of others from outside law enforcement and many officers do not value the mental health community (Patterson, 2004), the officers answering this survey seem to have positive perceptions of the mental health community.

The interdisciplinary nature of this corps of volunteers may affect perceptions of helpfulness. A program

---

9   Ibid, pages 355-356.

that draws from all levels of education and professional backgrounds may be the best way to provide services in a wide variety of crisis situations. The training, and contribution offered by someone with a background in social work might be quite different from that offered by someone with a psychology background. The fact that volunteers in this program work in pairs increases the likelihood that a victim can draw on multiple disciplines.[10]

Obviously, each Crisis Team member will conduct himself or herself differently.

What Kind of People Served on the Crisis Team?

Our Crisis Team operated at that time in a city with population of 199,564, of which:

> 61% were Caucasian, 28% Hispanic, and 9% Black; and 51% were female and 49% male. (U.S. Census, 2000). In 2008, the police force [had] more than 400 officers and [averaged] about 130,000 calls for service each year.
> Crisis Team volunteers (N=61 for the period studied) were predominantly Caucasian (85%) and female (80%); 13% were Hispanic and 2% Black. According to the application information available, 57% had a bachelor's degree in a mental health-related field, 38% had a master's degree (usually in counseling), and 5% had a doctorate; 54% had a background in psychology, and 18% had a background in social work. Other backgrounds included family studies and pastoral care.[11]

---

10   Ibid, page 357.
11   Ibid, page 351.

* * *

All in all, we concluded that in the darkest of circumstances, both officers and victims benefitted significantly from the immediate assistance provided by our Victim Services Crisis Team, as you'll read in more cases that follow.

CHAPTER FIVE
NOTHING LEFT TO LIVE FOR

"It did not really matter what we expected from life, but rather what life expected from us."[12]

—Viktor Frankl

Although many people find it extremely uncomfortable to talk about, the devastation of suicide can be felt everywhere. Through my work in Lubbock, I've personally witnessed its lethal tentacles assault the minds of men and women, young and old, rich and poor, the educated and illiterate, and individuals of various races; it is no respecter of persons.

According to a report published by the World Health Organization (WHO) in 2014:

> Every year more than 800,000 people take their own life and there are many more people who attempt suicide. Every suicide is a tragedy that affects families,

---
12 Viktor E. Frankl, *Man's Search for Meaning* (Boston, MA: Beacon Press, 1959), p. 77.

communities and entire countries; and has long-lasting effects on the people left behind. Suicide occurs throughout the lifespan and was the second leading cause of death among 15 to 29-year-olds, globally in 2012.

While the link between suicide and mental disorders (in particular, depression and alcohol use disorders) is well established in high-income countries, many suicides happen impulsively in moments of crisis with a breakdown in the ability to deal with life stresses, such as financial problems, relationship break-up or chronic pain and illness.

In addition, experiencing conflict, disaster, violence, abuse, or loss and a sense of isolation are strongly associated with suicidal behaviour. Suicide rates are also high amongst vulnerable groups who experience discrimination, such as refugees and migrants; indigenous peoples; lesbian, gay, bisexual, transgender, intersex (LGBTI) persons; and prisoners. By far the strongest risk factor for suicide is a previous suicide attempt.[13]

Responding to over 100 suicide calls during the past 15 years, I've likewise realized firsthand that many suicides happen impulsively in moments of crisis and that the strongest risk factor for suicide is a previous suicide attempt. Every verbal threat or mere thought of self-inflicted death that is expressed, no matter how casually or how often, needs to be taken just as seriously as any previously spoken idea of self-inflicted death. Nevertheless, one person's "I want to die tonight" can be very different from the next person's "I don't want to wake up tomorrow." When I hear those phrases, as a counselor, I quickly make an attempt to chase that thought down, see how tied to that thought this person is, and find out what that person might be planning to

---

13   See http://www.who.int/mediacentre/factsheets/fs398/en/; The World Health Organization 2014, Media Center, Facts Sheets, Suicide; accessed May 1, 2015.

do. He simply might be saying he's having a bad day. In another case, however, he might be adamantly determined to end his own life.

For those trying to grasp the reasons for suicide and distinguish between a person having a bad day and someone who is genuinely at risk, I recommend the book, *Night Falls Fast: Understanding Suicide* by Dr. Kay Redfield Jamison. Dr. Jamison is recognized as an international expert on depression, and is likewise personally familiar with the subject, as she writes:

> "I had tried years earlier to kill myself, and nearly died in the attempt, but did not consider it either a selfish or a not-selfish thing to have done. It was simply the end of what I could bear, the last afternoon of having to imagine waking up the next morning only to start all over again with a thick mind and black imaginings. … No amount of love from or for other people—and there was a lot—could help. No advantage of a caring family and fabulous job was enough to overcome the pain and hopelessness I felt; no passionate or romantic love, however strong, could make a difference. Nothing alive and warm could make its way in through my carapace. I knew my life to be a shambles, and I believed—incontestably—that my family, friends, and patients would be better off without me."[14]

* * *

Following are cases of people who, like Dr. Jamison, also came to "the end of what they could bear." At times, when I've arrived at such a scene, I have sensed that I could have made a difference; on other occasions, I have felt as if there was nothing I could have done.

---

14 Kay Redfield Jamison, *Night Falls Fast: Understanding Suicide* (New York: Knopf Doubleday Publishing Group, 2000) p. 290.

* * *

Late in the afternoon on Friday, March 29, 2002, I wrapped up my last class for the week at LCU, ran home for a quick bite to eat, and reported to the police department at 7:00 p.m.

Straightaway, my partner and I jumped into one of our unmarked patrol cars to begin our seven-hour shift, and although I really enjoyed my professorial work at the university, I was looking forward to a change in atmosphere. Almost immediately, a call came over the radio.

Someone had committed suicide.

Naturally, the police and EMS were dispatched to the scene.

Meanwhile, I decided that I'd drive by the victim's address just in case we were called to the scene…and we didn't have to wait too long. At 7:30 p.m. I picked up the radio and answered the dispatcher's call, "Victor 1, 34th and Q."

"Victor 1…280 requests you at…."

It was the suicide…my first suicide call.

When we pulled up outside the residence, the night was dark and windy—a fitting backdrop for the dismal scene we were about to encounter inside. My partner and I quickly gathered our referral papers, cell phone, and radio, and headed into the apartment building.

As soon as we entered the lobby, we met up with the ME, who was confused about the location of the residence. Fortunately, we were able to help him get his bearings, and then the three of us entered the elevator and traveled up a couple of floors.

It wasn't difficult to determine which apartment to go to next—a sergeant was standing at the front door. As the ME proceeded inside, the officer informed me and my counselor partner that instead of going inside, he'd like us to speak with a man who was a friend of the deceased and who had found him earlier in the evening. So, we headed back to the elevator in order to go downstairs and find the witness.

Once again, we stood and waited in the hallway, and the three of us made some small talk until the elevator, an extremely slow elevator, finally arrived. When the doors opened, we discovered the elevator was traveling up. At this point, the sergeant, who was ready to take care of business, turned to us and asked, "Do you want to go back and see the body?"

Thinking that I should probably be aware of what the man downstairs had found tonight, I said, "Sure," and we proceeded back down the hallway and into the apartment, where three officers were continuing to gather information and assist the ME.

My partner and I continued to follow the officer into a dining room/kitchen area, and that's where we came to a stop. Seated at a table was the man who had shot himself in the chest. I had never witnessed anything like it. Blood surrounded the hole gaping in his shirt, and his head was leaning back as far as I think it could possibly go. At the same time, his mouth was wide open—almost like he was groaning.

A revolver was still lying on the table in front of him, along with a couple of stacks of handwritten notes and what seemed to be personal papers. This man had placed towels and a fuzzy bathmat on the floor around his chair, which were now soaked in blood.

I watched the ME as he conducted some of his examination and listened while he deduced that this man had slowly bled to death as a result of shooting himself very low in the chest/stomach (which explained why he had time to put his gun down in front of him on the table).

After our brief inspection of the victim, my counseling partner, the sergeant, and I made our way back outside the apartment, onto the elevator, and traveled to a floor below. At this point, my partner was in need of a restroom. So the manager retrieved a key while the sergeant attempted to contact the witness downstairs on the phone.

There was no answer.

Meanwhile, I received a call on my radio, requesting counselors at another scene. In response, I informed Dispatch that we were 10-6 (busy) but would inform the station as soon as we were available.

Within the next few minutes, another officer remaining in the apartment upstairs called to us by radio and said, "Could you send one of those counselors back up here? His daughter is on the phone."

Once again, I headed for the elevator, and right before it closed, my partner managed to catch up with me. Trying to lighten the mood, I suggested we play "rock, paper, scissors" to determine whose job it would be to talk to the daughter. Then we got serious, and I asked my partner if she had any preference—should I handle the conversation, or would she? She opted for me.

A minute later, we walked once again into the apartment, and as soon as we entered, the officer holding the phone raised his eyebrows, showing an instant sign of relief. The very next second, he pointed to the receiver and whispered loudly, "This is his daughter," then handed it over to me (I'm still hoping to one day get him back for that maneuver).

"Hello. My name is Andy," I began, "and I'm a counselor with the police department. What have you been told so far?"

"They told me that my father is dead, but they didn't tell me how," the daughter said.

"Well," I began, "he killed himself tonight."

There was a pause, and I knew this devastating news was sinking in. Of course, I expected her to ask questions, and soon, she was able to talk.

"When did this happen?"

"Earlier this evening."

"Did anyone hear it?"

"I don't think so."

"How did he do it?"

"He shot himself."

"Where did he get the gun?"

"I'm not sure. ... Do you know if he owned any weapons?"

"I don't think so. ... Was it a .38 or a .44?"

I repeated the question to one of the officers, and he informed me that it was a .38.

"Yes, ma'am, it was a .38."

I could hear in her voice what I thought was some understanding, and she seemed to calm a bit. I didn't analyze her reaction. There could have been a hundred different reasons why it was important to know that the gun was a .38.

At some point during our conversation, I became acutely aware of the somber surroundings and the gravity of my responsibility. I was sitting behind a dead man, describing to his daughter the horrific actions he had taken, observing firsthand the police officers performing their job, and attempting to teach my partner to help a victim cope with such a grievous situation.

Then his daughter asked, "What happens now?"

I informed her of how soon she would be able to claim her father's body and when she would be allowed to enter the apartment. She seemed even more relieved once we determined that she didn't have to travel to Lubbock that night.

But then she realized that the daunting task of informing other family members was before her, and consequently, she needed more time to talk. And I was there to listen.

As we closed our conversation, I gathered some personal information from her, and she asked if I could leave a business card for her at the apartment. Our team's policy has always been to recommend other counseling resources rather than to promote any personal business as a member of the Crisis Team. Likewise, in this situation, I assured her that I would leave a referral sheet and a note promising that someone else from our counseling team would be contacting her later in the week.

She thanked me. I wished her well. We said good-bye.

After I hung up the phone, the officer, noticeably appreciative that I had taken care of the call, now wanted to talk. He admitted that he wasn't sure what he should say to the daughter, and we discussed the questions and the direct comments I made. I shared my view that, in situations like this one, it was best just to say what needed to be said and do so frankly.

The other officers and I then traded information, and to help all of us deal with the dismal situation, we chatted and joked around with one another. (I still smile when I remember one officer—he was uptight about a female EMS paramedic who had been recently calling him and wanted a date.)

While the officers continued to talk about all sorts of subjects, I got back on my radio and discovered that counselors were still needed at the other scene. After confirming the address, I informed Dispatch that we would be 10-76 (en route) within a few minutes. Our task here was done.

In the meantime, as a few of us were making our way out to the cars, I could hear an officer complaining, "I'm a mess. I've been looking through the DSM (Diagnostic and Statistical Manual of Mental Disorders), and I think I might have OCD…or maybe I'm bipolar…or I might be…."

"Just pick out one of 'em and get after it!" I called back over my shoulder. And everyone laughed as we headed off to our separate calls.

For the next several years, I would respond to many other suicide-related incidents—sometimes consoling family members after a loved one had taken his or her own life; at other times, I'd show up as a member of the negotiating team to talk to a person who was crying out for help.

My first call involving someone threatening to jump off of a bridge came when I was driving around town with my wife. Sergeant Ross Hester and Sergeant Mike Steen had been talking for an hour or two with a man standing on the guardrail of an overpass over Interstate 27. It was about 32 degrees on this foggy November night. This man's positioning was precarious even on a dry and normal day. He was standing as if he were on a diving board about to do a back dive. Wearing cowboy boots, he stood on the cement edge with his toes under the rail and his heels out in space as he faced the bridge deck, talking to these officers.

I believe it was Sergeant Steen who called and asked me to come over and pitch in. I turned to my wife and asked if she wanted to be dropped off at home first, but sensing the urgency of the call, she came along instead. After awkwardly making my way past the police cars blocking the freeway access road, I was directed to pull up right along the guardrail on which this man was balanced. I asked my wife if she was ok watching this, especially if the man decided to jump, and she said she was. So, I hopped out of my car and met with Sergeant Steen. He let me know how things had gone with this man; that he was upset over his wife threatening to leave him and taking their children from him. He may also have been drinking. He said they'd made the offer to him to talk with a counselor, and he accepted. I walked with Mike out onto the bridge deck and stood next to Sergeant Hester, who introduced me to this man. Once introductions were made, Sergeant Hester said that he and Sergeant Steen would step away so he could speak with me freely. I then found myself speaking one-on-one with this stranger who, at any moment, could decide to jump.

I never heard it myself, but other officers told me that the people who'd gathered along the freeway access road would periodically yell for this man to jump. I'm glad I didn't hear them because I felt enough pressure as it was. All I knew to do, as I began that conversation, was to rely on my counselor training. Be a calm, empathetic presence. Reflect back to him what he was saying so: 1) I would clearly understand him, and 2) he would know I was listening. Ask him clarifying questions, and possibly emphasize a direction he should consider. Be patient.

Sergeant Hester and/or Sergeant Steen would rejoin me and over the next few hours our conversation went through the same cycle—we'd listen to his troubles, he'd get to a more cognitive place, then he'd return to an emotional state. Over time he'd spend more time in the cognitive and it'd look like he was considering coming down from his perch. Then the emotions would return and we'd go again.

Finally he decided to come down. Unfortunately for him, being in that standing position for so long caused his knees to lock. When he shifted his weight to come down, he accidentally started to fall backwards. I distinctly remember him looking into my eyes as he fell backwards, grasping hand over hand for that guardrail. Sergeant Hester instinctively started towards him, so I put my hand on his shoulder and asked, "Are you sure you want to see that?" He stopped.

An EMS ambulance had been staged under our bridge, and the two medics sitting on the back of their ambulance heard the thud. They scooped this man up and took him to the hospital. I later learned that he'd only broken his hip/femur and was otherwise doing okay physically despite the 25 or so foot drop onto the freeway. The gallows humorist in me believes we should get credit for talking him out of jumping even though he fell.

I returned to my car that night and rejoined my wife. She had a perfect view of this man's attempt to grab the rail and subsequent fall, but was doing just fine. And she was fine with sitting there so long, watching to see how this would resolve.

I likewise was ok, but even now, I can still see the look of terror and helplessness in his eyes as he fell out of view. We had done the best we could, gave him our best for a number of hours, and couldn't think of anything we could've done better.

My most recent callout involving someone wanting to jump from a bridge came on August 30, 2010. In the last story we were on the 66th street overpass (pictured above). This time it was someone attempting to jump off the 42nd Street Bridge over Interstate 27.

Nothing Left to Live For

After arriving on scene in my own car, I swiftly made my way out onto the overpass (after having to explain to the deputies blocking traffic that it was okay for me to swerve around them), where I found and stood behind Officer Bryan Dubois, who was behind Officer Marcus Wall, the primary negotiator. They were already talking to a 31-year-old woman who had climbed over the wall, the railing, and was standing on the outside ledge over Interstate 27.

For the next hour, in 102-degree heat, the officers tried to reason with this woman who was very distressed with her personal circumstances. Several times, she stated she wanted to jump so she'd no longer be a burden to her family. Meanwhile, as time progressed, our team of four men standing together was able to make some progress and gradually move closer. Officer Wall tried to talk with her, but she was not interested in responding with much more than a few lines once and a while. Then all at once, the woman, who had been facing us, decided to turn her body outward and face towards the interstate below. This was not a good sign.

Immediately, I said to the officer in front of me, "I think she's gonna jump." I then walked over to Sergeant Nathan White and let him know what I thought. He got on the radio and let everyone know what was about to happen. Straightaway, Officer Wall attempted to distract her.

"Hey!" he spoke up a little louder. "Is that your husband over there?"

Luckily, this question did nab her attention, and she looked over in the other direction at a crowd that had gathered. At that very same instant, the three of us in line took a few quick steps toward her, when suddenly she looked back toward us again.

Instantaneously, the first guy stopped...so fast that each of us ended up colliding into the guy in front of us. And I was sure we looked like the incompetent Keystone Kops—you know, the ones in the silent films who are constantly running into each other. But we played it cool so she was none the wiser.

Then she said, "I don't see him over there."

"No...look. He's...*over...there*," Officer Wall repeated.

When she glanced that way the second time, the officers moved even faster, and as a MHP, I decided to stay where I was. I was fully aware that my job was not that of a cop. I don't arrest people. I don't shoot people. I don't put my hands on people. So, I stayed back—and "supervised" the scene.

Within the next several seconds, Officer Wall and other officers grabbed her and held her against the bridge wall/guardrail. Officer Wall grabbed the back of her pants, where a belt would be, and managed to come up with a fistful of underwear and pajama bottoms. In the midst of the commotion, this distraught woman decided to wrap her leg around the horizontal railing at the top of the wall/guardrail, and she had wrapped it really tightly.

I had seen this special technique before—the spider monkey trick!

Fifteen years prior, in 1995, after I had earned my bachelor's degree in Bible, I decided that I didn't want to be a pastor; and until I could figure out what I wanted to do, I went to work as a case manager and emergency child care worker at the intake center for the Children's Home of Lubbock (CHOL).

For the next year, I would often watch the evening news and see a story about some guy killing his girlfriend while there were three small children in the house. The next day, those kids would be in our care at the CHOL—one of the toughest jobs I would ever do. Being assaulted by little kids who desperately wanted to be back with their mom, caring for them daily, retraining them, bathing them, getting their poo wiped on me in retaliation, and all the while making $4.50 an hour was just not fun.

But now, standing on this bridge, I realized again that the difficult job at CHOL might actually have had its benefits. For it was while working at the children's home that I first witnessed the spider monkey trick—a tactic performed by a kid who didn't want to get out of the van which we used to transport them to the home. Specifically, he or she would curl one or more of their limbs around any object nearby, and hold on for dear life. It was a constant battle. In time, though, I learned how to successfully unwrap each arm and leg with some speed and expertise.

Now, watching the officers tangling with this woman, I thought, *I know how to handle this*, and without giving it much more thought (or asking permission), I jumped in and unwound her leg. The next moment, everyone kind of collapsed backward with the woman safe and in custody.

It did not go unnoticed that this ordeal might have ended much differently. Had the victim still been able to jump, she may have taken along an officer or two. With that thought in mind, the police department implemented a rope system and harness shortly afterwards. LPD patrol cars have a push bar, and we can use two patrol cars facing each other to attach one end of a long rope. Another rope would be hooked onto this long rope, with the other end on an officer's harness, ensuring he could move in various directions yet not get hauled out over the edge.

One final postscript to this story—on February 25, 2011, Officers Wall and Dubois were given the department's Life Saving Award for their work on the bridge that day. I was honored to receive a Certificate of Appreciation presented by the Lubbock Police Department and City Council for my counsel about the woman preparing to jump, and for my "prompt actions in assisting officers and preventing a person's immediate death." I owe it to the Children's Home of Lubbock and all those kids who trained me in the spider monkey trick.

* * *

When I heard about another person planning to jump off a bridge, this time the officers wouldn't need a rope, nor would I need to execute any arm or leg maneuvers. The police would choose to make use of another deterrent.

Once again, I was out cruising the city in our unmarked police car on a Friday night (this time solo) when I heard that a guy was on a bridge and threatening to jump off. When I pulled up to the site, all I could think about was getting up there as fast as possible so that I could deploy my negotiating skills with this guy sitting there on that ledge. But my adrenaline was pumping just a little too fast, so I knew I needed to chill first. It was 30 degrees, and I didn't want to jump out of the car without a jacket. What's more, there were four lanes of freeway access road between me and the situation…that, at first, I didn't take into consideration.

Once I made my way up safely to the bridge with a jacket, I could hear Officer John Hayes standing nearby talking to this guy who was sitting on the overpass and was likewise still facing the officer. Two other policemen were also present, one standing at each end of the guardrail, and a fourth, a sergeant, was supervising.

The guy on the bridge was very troubled, saying comments like, "My wife has left me…" and "She's going to take the kids." Meanwhile, I was impressed by Officer Hayes' natural ability for communicating understanding and empathy for this man.

Nothing Left to Live For

After a while, Officer Hayes noticed other EMS personnel who had pulled up and parked nearby and said to the man on the bridge, "Hey, why don't you and I head over toward the ambulance and get some help?"

The man agreed.

I stood there watching, relieved to see that this man was compliant and beginning to take a few steps in that direction, when all of a sudden, the two officers from either end of the guardrail quickly came in—and tased the man.

Oh no...this is not good, I thought. I had learned a few important tactics when attending negotiator training with the police department, and one piece of advice that especially stuck with me was: "Negotiate with a person as if you're going to see them again in another crisis situation." This meant that we should do everything possible to build trust the first time around in case there would ever be a next time. If, however, the subject felt that he had been lied to or mistreated in some way, any rapport or trust we had previously built would most likely be nullified.

With that training in mind, I assumed that in this case, the guy who had been on the bridge would now be totally irked that he had been tased, when it looked as though he was fully cooperating.

Meanwhile, the man was placed into the ambulance and the situation was secured. But as for me, I was struggling with the circumstances. So when the sergeant offered me a ride back to my city car that was parked below, I thought I ought to mention my concerns and see if I was missing anything.

"So, Sarge, why did you decide to tase this guy?"

"Well," he replied, "I told the guys that when we got him down off that guardrail, I wanted them to get him into custody as quickly as possible. I didn't want to take any chance that he might change his mind and jump anyway. So, I wanted them to tase him."

Made sense.

Still, I said, "Well, Sarge, you know, in negotiator school, they teach us to negotiate with a person like you're going to see them again."

He knew exactly where I was coming from and I could see he agreed. "So in this case, I think we better hope that this guy never gets the notion to jump off a bridge again, because he'll probably not trust that we'll keep the Tasers away the next time. And you know, from what I saw, he was compliant and walking to the ambulance willingly. We really didn't have a problem."

The sergeant looked at me and said, "Yeah, I guess you're right."

I understood his reasoning, and he understood my concerns. As a result, I asked what he thought about driving on over to the hospital to catch up with this guy and make sure everything was all right—that what was done, was done for his own protection. And the sergeant completely agreed.

In a short time, we arrived at the hospital, and when we located the man who had been standing on the bridge, we started out the conversation by mentioning that we were just stopping by to see how he was doing. Another point they emphasized in negotiator school was talking with people after the incident is secured; and it seems a great way to treat people. In the back of my mind I felt pretty sure that he would be upset and we'd have some damage control to do.

"So, how do you think it went tonight?" I got to the point rather quickly. "And what did you think about the officers tasing you?"

"Oh yeah," this guy looked at me and replied, "it made perfect sense."

Huh?

"I knew that the cops were worried about my safety, and I'm just glad they got me out of that mess when they did."

I couldn't have been more surprised or more wrong about his feelings on the matter. I wouldn't have blamed the sergeant for spiking the ball in my face after that, but he was gracious and only smiled.

Go figure. No harm, no foul. Sometimes, there's a guy who simply needs someone to show up and do something—maybe anything—to show that they care.

LPD SWAT Negotiators 2011 Team Photo

The primary negotiator, secondary negotiator, and supervisor working a call in the back of the LPD command RV.

* * *

I hadn't yet received a request to report to the scene, but this time, I decided to take the initiative and show up when I heard the dispatcher call out, "Suicidal subject—3000 block of the South Loop, eastbound."

I had been patrolling the city, driving around at about 9:00 p.m., when I changed direction and headed towards a lake area next to a business part of town. As I pulled up, I saw a small group of people standing near the water and realized that I was the first responder to arrive at the scene. Naturally, I stayed in the car and parked a little distance away. A minute later, two patrol cars pulled up right next to the scene.

At that point, I knew I could get out of the car, and as I drew closer to the group, I could see that a young man was on the ground, lying on his back. He was wrapped in some type of lightweight chain, probably about four feet long—the kind of chain that people often attach from their belt buckle to their wallet. Except…this guy had wrapped it around his neck a couple of times and was pulling on each end with both of his hands, attempting to choke himself.

Now, I'm not a physicist, but as I considered this object, the motion, the leverage involved, and the personal energy exerted in this situation, I was fairly certain that this young guy's attempt was not going to be successful. Nevertheless, his two friends—one young male and one young female—were thinking otherwise. Both were freaking out, yelling that he was going to die.

So as the officers were kneeling down next to the subject to begin the process of unwinding him, I walked over to the friends to see what I could do to calm them down.

"Could you tell me what's going on tonight?" I began.

Both the man and woman started to explain the events that had transpired before they decided to call 911. And eventually, they came to the point when I heard one of them say, "…and he's probably got a knife on him."

Straightaway, I stopped the conversation and made my way over to the officers, leaned in, and said, "Hey, the friends say he might have a knife."

Fortunately, one of the officers found and secured it right away, then went back to placing one of his knees on the guy's chest as well as pulling the guys' two hands together in an attempt to try and loosen the chain.

I started to turn away and walk back to the friends, but then I had to pause when I heard the guy on the ground complaining.

"Can you get your knee out of my chest?" he moaned to the officer. "I can't breathe!"

I loved the irony of his complaint. It didn't quite make sense…but all the same, it was funny, and yes, a few of the officers and I would joke about it later.

Certainly, we treated the young man and his matter seriously, but in a job where we face dark and depressing situations daily, our gallows humor has its benefits and comes in handy. Many EMS personnel, at some time, use this type of banter to help them cope with serious,

Nothing Left to Live For

stressful, and even life-threatening situations. It's a way to provide relief, cope, and strengthen our own morale.

Even Viktor Frankl, a survivor of four Nazi concentration camps, stated, "It is well known that humor, more than anything else in the human make-up, can afford an aloofness and an ability to rise above any situation, even if only for a few seconds."[15] He and a prisoner friend had determined to tell each other at least one humorous story every day.

Many times, people will watch television news coverage of a fire or a crime scene, and notice police officers or firefighters laughing. Some people will judge, and likewise be offended by these men and women, asking, "How can they laugh at something like this?"

It's very important to understand that these men and women deal with tragedy as a daily way of life. They are not laughing at the victim or the situation. They are attempting to rise above horrendous circumstances, using humor in order to cope and continue to do their job… or they'll simply go nuts.

Of course, there are times when there is absolutely nothing to find funny about a matter, like the call I received during the week of the Thanksgiving holiday.

I was at home when I was called by Dispatch to respond to a suicide. A 20-year-old female, still in the house, was refusing to leave the premises where her father had just shot and killed himself.

I had never dealt with a call exactly like this one, and on my way, I was thinking about what to say to encourage the young lady to come outside and talk to me. But by the time I arrived at the scene, the circumstances had changed (to be expected in any type of crisis and chaos). An officer had managed to talk her into leaving her bedroom via a window, and she was now sitting on the curb. So, I took a seat next to her.

"Do you want to tell me what happened?" I began.

"Well…my dad and I haven't seen each other for years. But not too long ago, he called and said that he wanted to come and spend some

---

15 Viktor E. Frankl, *Man's Search for Meaning* (Boston, MA: Beacon Press, 1959), p. 43.

time with me during Thanksgiving. So, I said, 'okay.' Then, tonight, when I was in my bedroom, I heard him calling out for me…and when I opened the door to come out, I saw him standing in the living room with a pistol at his head. It scared me, and so I hurried out and quickly closed the door. Then, when I opened the door again, he was still standing there with the pistol. So, I closed the door again…and that's when he pulled the trigger. I called 911, and the police were here right after that."

Throughout my crisis-counseling career, I have always tried to maintain my composure and cool, but as I heard this girl unfold what had just happened, I got to experience a new kind of reaction. I didn't feel compassion for the daughter, but rather anger towards her father. *What kind of person does something like this?* I thought over and over. And honestly, I was struggling. This young lady never mentioned her dad's last words—and I never learned if she was even interested in trying to understand why he shot himself in front of her.

Eventually, a few of her friends showed up on the scene, and I asked, "Do you have somewhere you can stay tonight?"

"Yeah, I can stay with my friends here," she responded.

"Well, do you need me to get anything from the house before you go?"

"Yes, I need my suitcase," and she listed some other items.

So, I went up to the officer at the front door and asked, "Is it possible for me to go inside so that I can get the daughter's suitcase and some of her personal belongings?"

"Sure," the officer said, "just don't kick the body."

I smiled as I moved on past him into the hallway area next to the living room and found the suitcase inside a built-in chest of drawers. And it was no wonder the daughter didn't want to retrieve it, because her Dad's body was lying very close by. In fact, I had to walk around his body to get to this specific piece of furniture. Still angry with the father, I paid attention to the officer's instructions and decided not to kick him.

Nevertheless, at the very next moment, when I leaned down to pull out the suitcase, I looked over at the body and saw this man's eyes wide open and seemingly staring back at me. Consequently, I felt this anger rise up inside of me.

Quickly, I grabbed the suitcase and a few other items, delivered them to the daughter outside, and helped her finish up with the police so that she could leave as soon as possible with her friends.

I left as well, but my struggle continued…and I was surprised at myself. I'm not an angry person, and I had certainly never been angry with a dead stranger before. And even as I returned home, this incident and a few questions hung on to me.

First, I asked myself, *Is it okay to be ticked off at someone who's dead?* Then I had to determine, *Is it okay to be furious with a dad who did this to his daughter?* And then, I experienced a theological malfunction and wondered, *Is God now disappointed with me for being mad at a dead guy?*

Fortunately, my wife and a pastoral friend listened as I explained my dilemma, and I was eventually able to work through it, just as I had worked through the emotions associated with my first suicide call. In this case, I decided that my infuriation made sense. Some people call it a "righteous anger." But whether or not I could justify such an emotion, what was more important, was the choice to release any resentment instead of holding on to it or to let it build. What helped me release the anger, both in this case and in the case of my first suicide call, was how I viewed it. These men made their choices, and God allowed things to transpire as they did, however wrong or hurtful these situations were in the short term. Still, I'll never forget the moment of looking into a dead man's eyes, feeling as though he was looking back at me, and being angry with him.

I likewise continued to think about the daughter. Typically, in the short amount of time that I spend helping victims at a crisis scene, I usually acquire only a snapshot of their lives. In this case, I learned that the daughter had been estranged from her father, she lived alone, and she was studying to be a nurse…and that's about the extent of what I discovered. Even when I asked if there was someone whom I could notify of her father's death, she declined the offer.

But I am not always spared that responsibility.

CHAPTER SIX
THE BEARER OF BAD NEWS

"No one loves the messenger who brings bad news."
—Sophocles, *Antigone*

One of my most difficult responsibilities as a member of the Victim Services Crisis Team (VSCT) has been to notify a parent, a spouse, a child…anyone…of the death of a family member or friend. There's just no easy way to tell a person that someone he or she loves, someone they are close to, has just passed away. A police officer or a VSCT member may be the ones to deliver a death notification, and it is possible to do so poorly. It's unfortunate, but it happens.[16]

As part of our crisis intervention training, each of our team members are advised that when faced with this daunting, at times overwhelming responsibility, our manner and language must always be most respectful to the deceased. (For example, using the deceased

---

16   For more about delivering death notifications, I recommend Janice Lord and Alan Stewart's book, *I'll Never Forget Those Words: A Practical Guide to Death Notification* (Compassion Press, 2008).

person's name is meaningful.) Likewise, we must be respectful to the person(s) to whom the message is given. As with any type of communication, we understand that how we deliver the message is just as important as what we say.

Even before we meet with the individuals or family members, we realize that it is extremely important to have all the facts straight—even the most difficult ones—and to have as much information as possible before speaking. One of the worst mistakes made is giving misinformation or using incorrect terminology.

Some people may accept the news quietly and not have much of anything to say, while others will ask several specific questions. A counselor's response, "I don't know…but will try to find out for you" is much more appropriate than taking a guess or giving a wrong answer. This is no time or place to get caught up in the throes of authority; our primary job here is to be empathetic and to show compassion.

At the same time, empathy doesn't mean that one should stammer and stutter and act as though giving bad news is the toughest thing they've ever done. Certainly, a person delivering the message needs to be gentle and considerate, but it is just as important to use plain and direct language without being abrupt. There is a fine balance here. Telling a long drawn-out story, using ambiguous language, keeping a family wondering what's coming up next, or giving them even a minute of false hope before you get to the truth, will increase the likelihood of poorly communicating information, not to mention increasing the suffering and pain.

The best way to deliver the message is to directly tell the truth with a genuine kindness, using a voice loud enough so that each one can hear you, starting with just the basic facts. "Your wife died in an accident an hour ago." "Your son shot himself in his bedroom this morning." "Your father was taken to the emergency room with chest pains and died of a heart attack." Most people appreciate the sincerity as well as the straightforward honesty, and a few have even thanked me.

Facts are a valuable commodity at these times. Unfortunately, in a crisis situation, facts are hard to come by. There have been times when a person was dead at the scene, but in the ER they got back a pulse. To date, I haven't told someone their loved one was deceased when they really were not. I pray that never happens.

Naturally, though, there are some people who just can't find it in themselves to deliver the heartbreaking news. I personally know of a few tough law enforcement officers who have struggled with this responsibility. Deep down, they have a big heart, and giving bad news is just not one of their strong suits. In such cases, a team made up of two officers, or an officer along with a MHP can decide which one is better equipped to present the hard facts and/or which one can provide additional information.

Once the family or friends receive the news, they will need space and time to absorb the shock. There is absolutely no room for impatience here as we listen and comfort the grieving victims, answer their questions, help them transition to what might be happening next, and inform them of decisions they might need to make. Meanwhile, it is important to keep personal opinions at bay and guard against judgments about how people should react or how they should grieve. Every individual deals with tragedy in different ways and in varying amounts of time (a topic covered more fully in the following chapter), which is evident as you read the details presented in the next three cases.

* * *

I was teaching a class at LCU in the middle of the afternoon and was just about finished when I took a call from Dispatch. The assistance of a Crisis Team member was needed at a residence where a 15-year-old female was reported to have shot and killed herself at home.

Realizing that the address given was only five blocks away, I immediately replied, "Mark me en route. I'll be there in three."

Then I looked back at 20 students and announced, "Class dismissed." And they silently rejoiced.

Feeling the urgency of the situation, I didn't take time to change into my polo shirt—the one labeled, "Victim Services Crisis Team" that I keep in my car with my negotiator shirt, bullet-resistant vest, helmet, and go-bag. Instead, I rushed out the door in my professor outfit, hopped in the car, texted my team to see if someone could meet me there, and was at the scene in a matter of minutes.

When I pulled up to the house located in a nearby residential area, I noticed that a couple of officers were already inside, and so I made my way over to a few teenagers standing in the driveway. They were obviously upset.

Introducing myself as a counselor with the police department, I said, "Can you tell me what's happened?" while trying to evoke a measure of calm with my tone and demeanor.

The kids began to pour out with much emotion the story of finding their high school friend now lying dead in her bedroom. Just a little while ago, she had texted them good-bye, mentioned something about killing herself, and then took a gun and pulled the trigger. These friends came rushing over to the house to find that no other family members were at home and that she had actually gone through with her intentions. Devastated, they called 911.

Sometime during my conversation with these youths, an officer quietly interrupted, "The parents have been contacted and are en route. They'll be here soon." Which also meant that one of the officers or I would be expected to notify this couple of their daughter's death. And yes, my stomach was in my knees. In the meantime, another VSCT member arrived and started visiting with the teenage friends.

Soon after that, a car quickly pulled into the driveway, and a man and woman stepped out. You could tell by their faces that they were mom and dad.

Stepping away from the teenagers, I joined an officer and stood quietly next to him. The news he gave was brief, and automatically, the mom dropped down into a sitting position on the pavement and just heaved forth with grief.

Immediately, I moved down beside her, while the father began to pace.

I sat there next to this grieving mother…perhaps for 20 minutes… and I didn't say a word. Every so often, the father would come over to where his wife and I were sitting and stand for several seconds. Then he'd anxiously move off to somewhere else. In time, I began to get the distinct feeling that he was thinking, *I just wish everyone would go away.* And I thought that perhaps, for these people, the best action might actually be for me and my partner to leave. I knew I could be wrong, but in case I was right, I wanted to honor that desire. Consequently, I turned to the mother and asked, "Would you like us all to leave?"

Turning back and pointing at me, she spoke with all earnestness through a stream of tears, "I don't know who you are, but I know you can help us. Please don't leave."

So, I remained…sitting there…silently sharing her sorrow…and wishing I could alleviate the father's pain.

Meanwhile, as in any case like this, where the death of a person occurs outside of a hospital, I was there to answer any questions, explain what was happening now, and what would happen next.

While a few of the officers continued their investigation inside the house, inspecting the scene, taking pictures, and writing their observations, one officer remained at the front door making sure that only official personnel went inside and out. If this family needed something from inside—depending upon what it was and where it was located—I would have done as I did in other cases, and obtained permission to go within the premises to retrieve and deliver that item.

This time, I likewise prepared the family for the arrival of the medical examiner (ME) and the mortuary service. When both arrived, the ME conducted his own investigation, and the mortuary service took possession of the body in order to transport it to the ME's office. The ME would eventually complete the rest of his investigation there, and then release the body to the family (or at the family's request, to a funeral home). The funeral director would, in turn, work with the family and help them decide what type of service would be scheduled.

Meanwhile, I stayed with the father…pacing…and the mother… sitting…there in that driveway.

Then…the area became very quiet. After about two hours, everyone else—the police, the ME, and the mortuary service—had come and gone. And now, the family could go inside.

Thinking about their daughter's bedroom, I realized that what the mother and father might see would likely traumatize them even further. Now my job was to do what I could to prevent that, and to offer even the smallest of help in order to eliminate what would be, for them, a most daunting task. And so, I offered, "How about I go in and check out your daughter's room?"

They both sincerely appreciated the offer, and accordingly, my partner and I went into the house and walked down the hall to where their daughter had shot herself in bed.

As we entered the room, we couldn't help but to immediately notice the blood-soaked bedding and mattress. Otherwise, not much seemed out of place.

Within the next few minutes, when we returned to the mom and dad, I said, "I think the best thing would be to get rid of all the bedding and the top mattress, and if it's okay with you, we'll take it to the dumpster right away." They agreed. So we did.

It was a humble task, but I could tell it made a difference to that mother…still collapsed in agonizing sorrow…and for the father…still pacing away in dreadful pain.

* * *

It was the middle of the night and cold outside, so I dressed in warm clothes. I had been responding to these types of calls for about eight years, and when I arrived at the address given, it looked like the typical homicide scene. Both ends of the street were blocked, and emergency vehicle lights were flashing. All types of civilians were milling around outside the stretch of yellow tape, while cops were moving in and out of a house—a picture I had witnessed many times before. Still, I knew that no crisis situation is ever exactly like any other, and as soon as an officer apprised me of the situation, I was certain that this one would be especially difficult.

A young mother of four children had just been killed by the estranged father, who had then also killed himself. Three of the children who had been in the house hadn't been harmed physically, and were being tended to by various officers. The grandparents (the mother's parents) had likewise arrived on the scene and were anxious to take immediate custody, but the police first needed to make sure that these people were who they claimed to be.

Meanwhile, I was also informed that the oldest child, a 12-year-old boy, wasn't yet aware of the tragic circumstances because he had gone to a friend's house for the night. Consequently, one of the officers asked if I would travel with a lieutenant to find this child, let him know what had happened, and bring him to the police department to meet up with his siblings. I agreed to go, and before I left, I informed the grandparents of the plan to find the other child and counseled with them a little.

Soon, we were off to an address where the police thought the 12-year-old was staying, and in the middle of a bleak, dismal night, the officer and I knocked on the door. When a woman finally answered, we asked if this particular boy was staying with her for the night. She answered that he was not, but fortunately, she knew where he was staying, and we were able to acquire the next address.

As to be expected, while we were standing there, she wanted to know, "What's happened?" and I immediately looked at the lieutenant for an answer. It was obvious that he didn't want to tell her but decided he should give her some brief information along with an admonition that she refrain from telling anyone until we could inform the boy.

Hastily, we returned to the car and moved on to the location—outside the city limits—to another house and another woman who came with a careful and guarded look to a mid-night knock at the door.

"Is Michael (not his real name) here?" the officer asked.

"What's goin' on?" she responded anxiously.

"Earlier tonight, the boy's parents died. And now, we need to take the boy to be with the other members of his family."

Even in the midst of the lieutenant's brief explanation, this woman started to lose it, and so the officer quickly went on to say, "Please let *us* tell the boy what has happened." But neither the officer nor I were confident that she had heard his last request, because when she went to the back of the house to wake the boy, we could hear her crying, and it was obvious that her voice was elevated.

We waited, hoping that the woman had not done too much damage, and within a minute or two, the 12-year-old boy came to the door with tears in his eyes. He was very still and very quiet as the officer explained that we needed him to join us in the patrol car so that we could take him to the police department to join his siblings. I decided to say nothing more until we were in the car.

Once we slid into the back seat and the lieutenant pulled away, I looked over at this child. But before I had a chance to begin, he looked back at me, and asked…

"What happened?"

"Tonight…your mom died."

All at once, his eyes and face simply crumbled into one of shock… and disbelief…and pain.

Then he turned forward, away from me…and wept.

After a few minutes, he attempted to get hold of himself, then turned to me again and asked…

"How did she die?"

"She was shot."

And again, there was that devastating look of shock…and disbelief…and pain.

He faced forward, and for the next few moments, his tears flowed uncontrollably.

Within another few minutes, again, he struggled to maintain control, then glanced back at me and asked…

"Who shot her?"

"Your dad shot her."

And upon this child's face was that intense look of pain...and disbelief...and more pain.

Then he turned away from me...and cried.

One more time, his eyes bravely met mine, and then he asked...

"What happened to my dad?"

"Your dad then shot and killed himself."

And this poor boy's heart, one more time, was filled with shock...and disbelief...and pain.

He cried again.

But still, he wasn't finished with his questions.

I could hear his fear as he asked about his three younger siblings.

"They're safe at the police department," I assured him. "Your grandparents will be coming to get them, and we'll also be there soon."

When we arrived a few minutes later, I stood back in awe as I watched this 12-year-old boy instinctively take his younger siblings under his wing and genuinely care for them. Then for the next several minutes, I talked with his grandfather, who admitted that the family knew that there was a problem, and they worried it would come to this. Moreover, they had tried to get some help, but obviously, it was not enough. As we parted ways, he thanked me for helping out that night.

These children, like so many, were left to cope with the trauma and the loss. As a mental health professional, I knew that they might block the incident or internalize it with grief and confusion, and more than likely, they would need counseling or therapy. Yet counselors face different challenges working with children, primarily because these youngsters haven't reached the level of emotional development to verbally communicate their feelings. And so, in my line of work, "play therapy" is often recommended—where children can express their feelings by using toys such as finger paints or a sand tray to portray what is going on in their lives. Children, like adults, will also often analyze a situation and blame themselves for not doing something to help. In this case, I knew this 12-year-old boy and his younger siblings would need friendly faces to surround them and people with whom they were familiar to talk to and provide stability.

Hence, it was most important to me that they be connected with their grandparents immediately.

And as you can see from my conversation with that young boy, giving a death notification is a hallowed thing.

* * *

Bad news is bad news any time of the year, but somehow, there's an added heartache when a tragedy occurs during a holiday. In years to come, what should be only a joyful occasion will most likely be tainted with a horrible and mournful memory.

Such was the case a few days after Christmas in the year 2008.

Late on a Saturday night, while everyone else in her family slept, a 15-year-old girl grabbed a set of car keys and drove away in one of her parents' vehicles. Picking up one of her girlfriends, then another, the three of them went out for a little spin. As she drove west on 114th street about 4:00 a.m., she didn't stop at a stop sign and unfortunately collided with another vehicle. Her one friend in the front passenger seat died at the scene. She and the third friend were taken to Covenant Medical Center where they were listed in satisfactory condition.

At approximately 4:30 a.m., I received the call. I was to meet a police sergeant near the home of the deceased girl and prepare to notify her family.

Soon, the sergeant and I met in the middle of the street. It was still dark, and he filled me in on the various details of the accident and all those involved. As we walked up to the front door, the officer then asked, "So…how do you want to do this? Do you tell them, or do I?"

"Well, in my experience," I said as we approached the front door, "usually the officer tells them what happened. You give them the facts… and I'll take it from there and try to pick up the pieces."

While we stood there waiting for someone to answer, we couldn't help but notice that the doormat read, "United States Marines." Then…

The Bearer of Bad News

we knocked again…and we waited. It wasn't yet five in the morning, and it was no surprise that we would have to knock again.

Eventually, someone came to answer, and the door slowly opened.

It was obvious to us both that this man was the father, and likewise evident, was that he had been sleeping. Nevertheless, when he realized that a police officer and another guy in some type of uniform were standing at his door, we had his attention, and he asked us to step inside.

"Is this the residence of (and we gave his daughter's name)?" the sergeant asked.

"Yes…but she's in the back sleeping," the father said with conviction.

Quickly, I spoke up. "Well, will you go back to her bedroom and make sure she's there?"

"Because there's been a traffic accident tonight…" the sergeant added.

"And we want to make sure she's here and not part of the accident," I finished.

The father looked at us as though he was certain that we were wrong. Even so, he went to the back of the house, and as we waited, we could hear him trying what was obviously the bedroom doorknob. We also knew by the sound of it, that he had found it locked.

Within the next few seconds, we heard the thrust of his body upon that door and then…this scream of grief.

At that same moment, two young men in their late teens or early twenties, who I assumed to be this father's sons, woke up and came out to us, along with the father. And for all three, the sergeant quickly laid out what had occurred earlier that morning.

"There's been an accident. Your daughter was traveling with two other girls. She was sitting in the right-front passenger seat, and she died at the scene."

Once again, the father, as well as the boys, let out a grief-stricken yell. And as one of the boys threw a punch into the wall, the father looked up toward the ceiling and yelled, "F… You, God!"

I was surprised by the reaction, but at the same time, I wasn't. I realized that the father, most likely a Marine, was recognizing who was in charge of life and death, and he went straight after Him.

By this time, the mother was now also awake and came to the hallway as well. Her reaction, though, was completely different. She seemed to be calm and was able to talk to us, yet she didn't ask a lot of questions.

Quite aware of the three very angry and grief-stricken men standing next to me, I opted to look towards the mother and ask her directly, "Is there anything I can do here? Is there anything I can do for you?"

"No. It's best that you leave," she replied. "I can take care of this."

And so we said good-bye. But I'll always remember this father's painful shock and his subsequent outpouring of emotion. Denial cannot remove the sting of a bitter truth. And he had been so certain that the bad news just couldn't be true.

CHAPTER SEVEN

"THIS CAN'T BE TRUE"

"Reality is merely an illusion, albeit a very persistent one."
—Albert Einstein

People's reactions to personally tragic circumstances are as numerous and as different as the victims themselves. As I've responded to hundreds of crisis situations and talked with a multitude of people trying to deal with heartrending and overwhelming circumstances, I've become fully aware that there is no *common* or *natural* way to react to an *uncommon* or an *unnatural* situation. Anything can be expected. Yet, Viktor Frankl, the Austrian psychologist who survived many atrocities while imprisoned in four Nazi concentration camps, put it this way: "An abnormal reaction to an abnormal situation is normal behavior."[17]

Many people assume that the "right" way to respond to a tragic accident or to the news of a loved one's death is to show some form of grief or sadness. But each individual can express that grief and sadness in a myriad of different ways. At the same time, some people will also

---

17   Viktor E. Frankl, *Man's Search for Meaning* (Boston, MA: Beacon Press, 1959), p. 20.

display bitterness or anger. Others will recoil and deny the truth, although evidence is right in front of their eyes. I've even sat with people who scoff or laugh in disbelief. And once in a while, I've dealt with a few who exhibit a quiet acceptance. Through the years, I've learned to prepare for most any type of demonstrative and emotional outpouring, as well as something more ambiguous and restrained. Occasionally, though, I've been taken off-guard, as happened when I was subjected to a lecture by a girl in high school.

I was at home, helping to care for my newborn baby girl, when the police called me to come down to the station to speak with a mother. She was a 16-year-old high school girl who had just lost her own baby.

When I arrived within the next 30 minutes, a detective was still in the process of interviewing her, and when he finished, I took a seat in his office to see how I could help.

After I introduced myself, I discovered this girl was currently living in an orphanage. Her baby was also living there, that is, until this morning. I wasn't aware of the circumstances of the child's death, but I did know the mother was not being charged with any crime. My job was to now offer empathy as well as to listen to her concerns and answer any questions I thought she might have about what happened next.

But rather than seek comfort or ask for information, this young girl began to admonish me with a calm and cool lecture, saying I should cherish my own children. As I listened, her words didn't seem to be coming from a place of wisdom but perhaps from a place of young grief. Her conversation wasn't flippant or wrong—just kind of awkward, and her advice struck me as a little odd.

But no matter how peculiar I thought her words were, I likewise knew they were in reaction to an *abnormal* situation (the death of her own baby), and at this moment, this was her *normal* behavior. Hence, I had no right to consider her words or deeds as otherwise. Who knows? She may have been speaking aloud to herself rather than directly at me. In any case, I wasn't "walking in her shoes," and I knew next to nothing of her past or present circumstances. It wasn't my place to pass judgment or hold her accountable. The same holds true about any other victim in any other emergency or crisis situation, even when it's obvious that the danger or pain has been self-inflicted.

As we continued our conversation, she didn't seem to be heartbroken, and for some reason, I didn't expect her to be. Thus, she was able to ask and answer cognitive questions. Her judgment and perception seemed to be intact, as opposed to many victims who are, at first, often extremely emotional and not able to reason or make sense of what is happening during such a difficult and trying time.

I believe a person cannot simultaneously respond both emotionally and cognitively as they attempt to deal with what may be the worst day of their lives. They certainly can flip back and forth between the two from moment to moment. In some cases a person will be consumed with emotions such as grief, sadness, anger, or bitterness. After a while, he or she may then begin to mentally process what has happened, and also be able to ask and answer questions. Some additional time will pass, and the same person will become emotional once again. Then, after a while, he or she will be able to quietly reason and make some additional decisions. A person can continue to flip back and forth between these two states—cognition and emotion—for varying lengths of time, sometimes very quickly, as they attempt to handle an abnormal and traumatic situation.

Meanwhile, my task is to simply be there for those persons, supporting them and allowing them to experience both states of mind at their own pace. In situations where an accident or a death has occurred, I will attempt to help them find a place of calm so they can eventually answer questions and provide the necessary information in order for the police and other emergency services personnel to effectively do their job. In addition, I want to help the victims understand as best as possible what has just happened and give them some advice as to how they can get through the next hour. I also try to provide a place for catharsis—an emotional outpouring and release. It's an art, not a science, determining which is most beneficial: allowing catharsis or helping them move to a more cognitive state. Helping someone navigate the waters of crisis is more difficult when I personally know or have some type of relationship with the victims.

In chapter 2, I described the time when I was instructed by the chief of police to meet with a room full of SWAT officers immediately after the accidental death of one of their teammates. You may recall that I decided to conduct just a short demobilization and was extremely uncomfortable doing so, especially because I knew these officers were not interested in being "demobilized." After I entered the briefing room and quickly offered some basic coping measures, one of the officers angrily asked, "Are you done?" to which I meekly responded, "Yes, sir."

That officer then demanded, "I need all non-sworn personnel to exit this room." I immediately left, wishing I could have offered something more to those men. At the same time, I didn't take this particular officer's conduct toward me as a personal affront. It was obvious that he was speaking from a place of frustration and even grief, and there was no reason for me to be offended.

During the next few years, as I became more engaged with the police department on a professional level, I also became involved with some of the officers on a social level. At one point, when a few guys heard I'd played hockey in high school, they invited me to join their pickup league. Ultimately, this activity helped to build relationships, and after a few games I earned some respect as a goalie, even from the guy who, years earlier, made it clear that he wanted me out of that briefing room.

Sergeant Chris Breunig played offense on the hockey team, and he and I became friends. Occasionally, we, along with our wives, would go out to dinner or see a movie. One evening, when the four of us were out together, I thought it was time to bring up the subject. I figured we'd need to get all our cards on the table.

"So…Chris, do you remember that day Kevin died, in the briefing room afterwards, when a bunch of SWAT officers were getting ready to go home?"

"Yeah, I remember that," he answered with a slight emotion in his voice.

"And do you remember being introduced to a tall, skinny, mental health guy who came in to say a couple words before you left?"

"Mm-hmm."

"And...do you remember who that guy was?"

Chris paused, then raised his head, and looked directly at me. I could see the wheels turning and his facial expression let me know it hit him.

"Oh man, Andy. What did I say?"

"Well, if I remember correctly, you said you needed all civilians to leave the room—or something like that."

Chris started to apologize all over the place, and he was effusive. I finally broke in and said, "No, no, dude...you didn't hurt my feelings. I just figured if we're gonna keep on dating and go anywhere with this relationship, we better clear the air." And then, we laughed.

I never forgot Chris' reaction that day, yet because of his frustration or sorrow or whatever it was, he wasn't able to remember what he had said, or to whom he had said it. Nor could he recall that he had basically kicked me out of the room. Meanwhile, that day, I had been praying, "Oh, God, help me not make this worse."

As the officers and I got to know each other, any tension subsided, and we became friends in many cases. I was grateful my prayer had been answered.

Since then, I have dealt with hundreds of crisis situations, realizing that neither I, nor anyone else should hold something against another person for what they say or do in the moments and hours immediately following a chaotic and stressful situation (unless, of course, it's something reprehensible like rooting against the Seattle Seahawks). Furthermore, while there are people who make all kind of remarks, there are just as many victims who aren't able to say anything at all and sometimes not able to move. Most often, it takes a person a while to adjust to reality.

* * *

Shortly after the ringing in of the New Year in 2008, in the midst of a 20-degree night, a 56-year-old woman was walking along a dark, two-lane road, inside Loop 289, in Northeast Lubbock.

She and her male companion had been traveling in a truck and started to argue.

Eventually, she became so upset by the conversation that she demanded he pull over. She then exited the truck and began to walk west toward the city, on the left-hand side of the road, into oncoming traffic.

The male driver, also headed west, soon pulled up along the shoulder, across the road from her. He rolled down his window, asked her to get back inside the vehicle, and go home with him. She agreed, and he was relieved to see her begin to take a step across the road.

But the next second, he couldn't believe—he didn't want to believe—what happened right in front of his eyes.

All of a sudden, she was flying through the air, and in an instant, she was thrown alongside the road. A car headed eastbound had hit her.

Eventually, I arrived at the scene.

Following is a transcript of the conversation between a police officer, who first arrived on the scene, and the male victim, which is followed by my dialogue with this same man.

Notice three observations.

First, as the officer begins to ask cognitive questions, such as, "What is your name?" and "What is her name?" he *waits for several seconds* for each response. More often than not, the distraught man does not answer.

During these moments, most likely, his emotions of grief and shock are interfering with his memory and state of cognition. In his condition of despair, he may not hear what the officer is saying, or he may not understand what the officer is saying. Or it could be that he may have temporarily forgotten the answer, or he simply cannot answer. However, at the same time, the officer needs to collect important information as quickly as possible. The officer is also aware that if he insists that the grief-stricken man give immediate and complete answers, he will very likely compound this man's stress, which will result in a further delay of acquiring the necessary facts.

Over time, as the officer, and then I, continue to ask cognitive questions, the victim is able to answer briefly—sometimes very briefly. This phenomenon demonstrates what I mentioned earlier, that victims might go back and forth from an emotional to a cognitive state, eventually remaining in the cognitive state longer and perhaps even capable of expressing a few sentences. As you read the transcript, notice the clock hour and minute designated at certain parts of the conversation. This is my attempt to reveal the amount of time that passes and the patience that is exercised as we try to help this man.

Second, notice that I've underlined how many times the distraught man says, "It can't be true," or "No, no, no," or some form of denial of the event. I haven't counted the number of times he makes such a statement, but I know it is several.

Third, a person in a state of shock and grief should not be held responsible for their *first* answer to a question. In this case, when I ask the despondent man, "Is there anyone I can call?" He says, "No." Later on, at the police department, however, he reveals his brother's name—a brother who lives in town. When he answers, "No," the first time, is he lying to me? No, he is not lying. Rather, he simply isn't able to answer the question. Thus, it is perfectly logical to ask the same question a few times. Many people can answer at some point.

Likewise, after an individual has calmed down, he or she may change the details of their story. Does this mean they first neglected to tell the truth on purpose? No. Although some people will lie at the scene of a crime or accident, most people, after being bombarded with chaos and confusion, simply need some time to think. After they go home, or once they calm down and the emotions subside, they might be able to recall some additional information. Their brain kicks in, and they are able to more clearly reflect on what has happened. So, it is often sensible to give a victim 12 to 24 hours for the adrenaline to settle down. Note that many police departments will also allow an officer involved in a deadly force incident to wait 24 hours before giving his/her statement about the traumatic experience. These departments realize that adrenaline, fear, and memory don't mix. Therefore, when a witness is required to give a statement, we need to be patient and give them a chance to recall exactly what has happened. If we can respect this phenomenon, and give the victim time to process, we will also be able to honor and meet the need by the police to acquire factual information.

In my classes, I give essay exams that require the student to learn a lot of information and then keep it in their mind. Unfortunately, the stress of the exam interferes with memory, and I watch students hit their head trying to get the memory to come out. Once the stress passes, usually out in the hall, far from the anxiety of the exam, they find the missing memory and let out the appropriate sighs, gasps, and appeals to God.

In the following transcript, which was taped by a video camera in the patrol car, "O" designates the Officer's words. When the grieving man does respond, his answer or statement is designated by the word "Answer." I've watched this video and listened to the audiotape many times, and I'm always struck by the officer's exceptionally courteous tone and kind voice as well as his extremely patient manner as he deals with the victim.

* * *

At 12:35 am on January 1st, 2008, the grief-stricken man is on his knees, kneeling and sobbing over a woman who has just been hit by a vehicle traveling about 50 miles per hour and is lying on the side of the road. The immediate area is very dark, while a stretch of lights from the city of Lubbock can be seen in the distance. The flash of strobe lights is all around. EMS can be heard approaching and then arrives. A police officer is bending over next to the sorrowful man and begins to ask him questions. The following exchanges move pretty slowly:

"This Can't Be True"

O: What happened, sir?...

O: Sir, what's your name?...

O: Sir, I gotta talk to you...

O: They got to work on her...

O: Please, sir, step away so they can...

O: Please, sir, step over here... Okay?... Okay?...

O: Step over here, sir... Okay?...

O: So they can help her...

O: Sir, can I talk to you over here?...

O: Please step away so they can help...

O: What is your name?...

O: What is your name, sir?...

O: What is her name?...

O: What is her name?...

(The man kneeling along the road continues to sob, now holding his knees and rocking back and forth.)

O: What is her name?...

(The man kneeling mumbles and cries.)

O: Say what?...

(The EMS staff is now placing the injured woman into the ambulance. As they do, the man allows the policeman to help him up. Together, they walk a few steps away. Patrol car and ambulance lights continue

101

to flash, and radio dispatch can be heard in the background. The man continues to sob with grief.)

O: I wanna get some information from you. Is that all right?...

O: Is that all right?...

O: Sir, you gotta calm down so I can talk to you...

O: I gotta get some information; I'd like to talk to you about what happened. It'll take a few minutes. I need you to think things over. All right?...

O: What's your first name?...

O: What is your first name, sir?...

O: What is your first name?...

Answer: [The man mumbles his first name].

O: What is her first name?...

O: What is her first name?...

Answer: (incoherent mumbling).

O: Was it just you and her out here walking?....

O: Just you and her?...

(The officer cannot understand the man as the man continues to cry.)

O: Where were you walking to?...

O: Were you in the car?...

O: Were you in the car with [the officer says what he thinks is the woman's name]?...

O: Do you have a jacket?...

O: Do you have a jacket to wear, sir?...

Answer: Oh my God, oh my God, oh my God. (The man continues to cry.)

O: Sir, I gotta talk to you. We need some information. All right?...

O: Okay?....

O: Do you have a jacket?...

O: Is it in the truck?...

O: In the truck?...

O: Did you get into an argument?...

O: Were you headed back home?...

O: Do you have a driver's license on you?...

O: Can I see it?...

O: Can I see your license, sir?...

O: Do you have a license on you?...

O: Can you get it for me?...

O: They are taking her to University Medical Center. What's her name?...

O: Is it [the officer says three different women's names]?...

O: And your name?...

Answer: [The man says his name].

O: How old is the woman?...

Answer: Fifty-five or fifty-six. Oh my God, Oh my God. <u>This can't be true</u>.

O: You were married to her, right?...

O: This gentleman needs some information from you…

O: Her name is [officer says a woman's name]?...

Answer: Yes.

O: Are you married or not married?...

O: Do you know her birth date?...

Answer: Don't know.

O: Did she have any medical problems?...

Answer: No.

O: Is she married to you?...

O: Girlfriend?...

O: How do you know her?...

O: Are you living together?...

Answer: Yes, four or five years…

O: And where do you live at?...

Answer: [The man gives his address].

O: Do you have a driver's license?...

O: Can I see that?...

"This Can't Be True"

(The man finds his wallet and hands his driver's license to the officer.)

Answer: Oh my God, oh my God.

O: I won't ask you any more questions now...

O: I think there is a credit card here. Okay, I got it. Here's the license. ... Sir, do you want to get in my car for the heat?...

O: We don't want you to freeze to death out here. We want you to get warmed up for now...for a few seconds...

(It is now 12:50 a.m.—15 minutes has passed since this policeman showed up at the scene of the accident and began to ask questions. At this moment, the man is crying very hard, and he continues to sob, "Oh my God. Oh my God. Oh my God...." The ambulance and three patrol cars with lights flashing remain parked on the road.)

O: Mr. [name], can you tell me what you were arguing about?...

O: Why did she ask you to stop the car?...

O: Were you arguing?...

Answer: (The grieving man nods his head.)

O: About what?...

O: What happened when...?

Answer: <u>This can't be true. This can't be true.</u> ... She was walking, and I was driving up.

O: Were you trying to get her back in the truck?

Answer: She was walking on that side. I pulled over on the other side.

O: Did you have anything to drink tonight? At a bar or at home?

Answer: Yes, at the house. … Oh my God. <u>This can't be true.</u>

O: We need you to think about what happened…

O: You were arguing about…what?

Answer: <u>I just can't believe it.</u>

(At this point, the officer moves his patrol car. He pulls it off the road and onto the shoulder. Directly in front of the police car, several feet away, sits the man's truck. Lights from surrounding emergency vehicles continue to flash. The distressed man has not yet put on any coat. He is dressed in a long-sleeved shirt and jeans. He is now sitting in the back of the police car. Once in the car, the man begins to sob again and cries, "Oh my God.")

O: Where do you work at?...

O: Do you work around here?...

O: Where do you work at?...

O: What were you arguing about?...

O: Were you drinking?...

O: Were you arguing about something at the time?

Answer: We were arguing about…I bought life insurance for my ex-wife. … Oh my God… (The man is sobbing and groaning.)

O: Mr. [name]…

Answer: Oh my God. <u>No. This can't be true.</u> Oh my God.

O: Mr. [name], someone is coming here to talk to you.

Answer: <u>This can't be true. This can't be true. This can't be true. This can't be true.</u>

O: Mr. [name], do you have a contact or phone number at your house?

Answer: No.

O: Do you have a cell phone?

Answer: No.

O: Do you have any phone?

Answer: No.

O: Does [the woman's name] live with you?

Answer: Yes.

O: At the same address?

Answer: Yes.

(At this point of the conversation, it is almost 1:00 a.m., approximately 25 minutes since this policeman arrived on the scene and started to talk to this man.)

O: Do you know her birth date?

Answer: <u>This can't be true. This can't be true.</u>

O: Is that her picture right there?...

O: Is that her picture right there?...

O: Okay. ... That's her?

Answer: Yes. I believe her birth date is [the man gives a date]. ... Oh my God, <u>no, no, no</u>. Oh my God. <u>This can't be true.</u>

O: Does she work anywhere?...

O: Where does [the woman's name] work at?...

O: Mr. [name], where does she work at?...

Answer: I can't remember. … <u>No, no, no</u> (groaning). <u>This can't be true.</u>

(The man starts to get out of the police car.)

O: Mr. [name], please stay back there in the car for now. This is a crime scene right now…or an accident scene. Stay right there for me. Stay right there for me, okay?...

(The officer gets out of the car to talk to another officer. The man in the back seat quiets down when the officer is out of the car. In a few seconds, the disheartened man also gets out of the car and walks toward the officers. This man then walks aimlessly for a few steps as the officers are having a discussion and pointing to various locations. In approximately one minute, the same officer who had been talking to this man escorts him back to the police car. The man gets in the back seat of the car once again. It is now 1:04 a.m.)

O: Mr. [name], could you put your feet in the car?...

O: Please sit back real quick, okay? Watch your feet. … A little bit more. (The officer continues to help the man get in the back seat of the car. Nothing is said for approximately one minute. At this point, the only vehicle that can been seen parked in front of the patrol car is the man's truck. Two other men continue to walk around on the road, shining flashlights on different spots. The grieving man is sitting alone in the back seat of the car, looking out the window at some of his wife's things, and he begins talking to himself.)

Answer: <u>This can't be true. No. No. No. This can't be true.</u>

(It is 1:08 a.m. when I arrive at the scene as a Victim Services Crisis Team counselor. I have very little information as I begin this conversation. I slide in the back seat of this patrol car, on the side next to the shoulder of the road. The man who is crying doesn't look at me but stares out the window towards the middle of the road. He seems to have calmed down. Even so, because I'm sitting in the back of a patrol car with someone I've never met, I need to be aware of my own safety. Hence, I place my foot where I can keep the door open as well as prevent it from locking, and thereby make a quick exit if this man gets angry with me. What's more, the prisoner shield and my extra-long femurs do not mix. Consequently, I am forced to sit in an awkward sideways position for the entire conversation.

You will notice that my words, throughout the remaining transcript, are preceded by an "A:" representing "Andy." At several places, I have inserted the hour and minute of the conversation, to give a more accurate picture of the length of the conversation, including the words and the times of silence. Very rarely is the conversation continuous. There are often long pauses between one question and another. I try to have a calm and caring tone as I ask questions. As I begin to talk to this man, I can see three policemen standing and talking in front of the car.)

1:08 a.m. – A: Sir, my name is Andy. (The man breaks down and cries again as I start to speak.) The police asked me to come and see if there is anything I can do for you.

Answer: <u>This couldn't have happened</u>. Oh my God (The man cries out with a growling-like sound, then mumbles in pain. I allow him to cry, and I am quiet for approximately one minute.)

1:09 a.m. – A: Sir, this sounds like a horrible accident.

Answer: Oh my God. What am I gonna do now?

A: (I'm not inclined to answer his question. It seems too early to tackle this.) Do you have any family in town?

Answer: Yes.

1:10 a.m. – A: Have you talked to them?

Answer: No.

A: Who do you have here in town?

Answer: Her family—yes. ... We've been together five years.

A: Where do you guys live?

Answer: (The man's answer is incoherent, and he cries even harder.) ... <u>This can't be true. This can't be true.</u>

1:11 a.m. – (I am quiet for about 60 seconds while he cries.)

Answer: God, what am I gonna do? Oh my God. <u>No, no, no, no. This can't be true.</u>

A: Do you wanna go back to your house?

Answer: I gotta go find her family.

A: Where do they live?

Answer: (He mumbles.)

A: Right there next to you?

Answer: Yes. ... Oh my God. <u>No. This can't be true.</u>

A: Who is there?

Answer: Oh my God, oh my God, oh my God. <u>This can't be true.</u> Oh my God. Over a stupid, little argument.

(There is nothing said, and all is quiet for the next 60 seconds or so.)

1:13 a.m. – A: Was the argument what led to her getting out of the car?

Answer: Yes. ... Oh my God. <u>No, no, no.</u> Oh my God. <u>I can't believe this, no.</u>

(The man is now taking very heavy breaths.)

Answer: <u>No, no, no, no.</u> ... She was dead, wasn't she?

A: What?

Answer: She was dead, wasn't she?

A: Yes, sir.

Answer: She was dead.

A: That's what the officer said to me. ... Did they take her to the hospital anyway?

Answer: Yes, but she was dead already. ... She was dead already.

1:14 a.m. – A: You know you didn't cause this, right? This was a horrible accident.

Answer: No. ... She stepped right out in front of the car.

A: Oh, you saw it?

Answer: Yes. She stepped...

A: She didn't see it coming?

1:15 a.m. – Answer: Yes. ... I had already pulled over. The car was coming ... and the car pulled over in that lane. I guess the car didn't see her. I saw when the car hit her. ... Oh my God. (The man sobs.)

A: But you were right there with her.

Answer: If she would've just stayed in the car. ... all because of a stupid argument. ... Oh my God. Oh my God. Oh my God. Oh my God...

1:16 a.m. – A: Let me go see what we can do about getting you home. Be right back, okay?...

(I step out of the car to ask an officer when this man can go home. I see the woman's shoes and purse still lying on the side of the road. I am gone for less than a minute, and while I am out of the car, this man continues to sob and grieve out loud.)

Answer: Oh my God. Oh my God. Oh my God. Oh my God.

(I return to the car and slide into the back seat once again.)

1:17 a.m. – A: Sir, there are accident investigators out here, and one of the investigators is going to need to talk to you before you go home. So, it's going to be a while longer.

(There is no answer, and all is quiet for 30 seconds. Then, the man cries out loud…)

Answer: <u>No, no, no.</u> … I want to go home.

A: I know you do.

Answer: God, <u>I can't believe this. I can't believe this</u>. (He continues to sob for another minute.)

1:19 a.m. – Answer: <u>This can't be true. No, no, no, no, no, no, no, no.</u>

(I am quiet while the man continues to cry.)

1:20 a.m. – Answer: Let me go home. Just let me go home. Let me go home. Let me go home.

(I am quiet.)

1:21 a.m. – Answer: Oh my God. Oh my God. Let me go home, please.

A: Do you understand about an officer having to interview you before you go?

(This man speaks to the police officer sitting in the front seat.)

Answer: Can I go home?

O: What, sir?

Answer: Can I go home? Can I please go home?

O: We're gonna try to get you out of here as soon as we can. An officer out here needs to talk to you. He's already out here, but he's got to take a look at the scene real quick. Okay?... We've got to get a statement from you about what happened, all right?... Before you go home.

(The man is quiet for a few seconds. Then he cries out again...)

1:22 a.m. – Answer: Oh my God. Oh my God. <u>No, no.</u> ... I just wanna go home.

O: I understand...and I'm not gonna hold you here any longer than I have to. Okay?...

(At this point, the camera in the patrol car is turned and pointed at the grieving man and me in the back seat. The man is crouched very low in the seat. He continues to stare out the window and wipe his eyes. He can see her personal items scattered on the road. I look at him every few seconds.)

Answer: <u>I can't believe this. This ain't true. This ain't true. This ain't true.</u>

A: Who is there at your house tonight?

Answer: Nobody.

A: You said your in-laws live near you?

Answer: <u>No.</u> ... Oh my God. <u>This can't be true. This can't be true. This can't be true.</u> Oh my God. Oh, <u>no, no, no.</u> ... <u>No, no, no.</u> (His hands cover his face.) <u>No, no, no.</u> (He beats his fists into his legs.)

1:23 a.m. – Answer: What am I gonna do now? What am I gonna do now?

1:24 a.m. – A: (Again, I am not inclined to tackle these questions right now.) Where is your family?

(No immediate response.)

Answer: Oh my God. Oh my God. Oh my God. Oh my God. <u>This can't be true. This can't be true. This can't be true.</u> (His hands are covering his eyes. He continues to sob.) Oh my God.

(I am quiet for a minute and continue to look over at the man every few seconds.)

1:25 a.m. – Answer: Let me go. Please let me go.

A: They just need to hear from you before you go.

Answer: Oh my God. <u>No</u>. (He is shaking his head and now heaving.) Oh my God. (He is leaning his head on the window.) Oh my God, <u>no, no.</u> (His shoulders continue to shake up and down with grief.)

(I am quiet for another minute.)

1:26 a.m. – Answer: Sir, please let me go.

A: Mr. [name], is there anyone who can stay with you tonight?

Answer: No.

A: Have any friends [or] family that you need me to call?

Answer: No.

A: Anybody that you work with?

Answer: No.

1:27 a.m. – A: Somebody that I can call that can meet us at your house?

(The man leans back into his seat, then leans his head onto the window, then rocks back and forth.)

Answer: Oh my ... let me go.

1:27 a.m. – A: You'll be able to, once they talk to you.

Answer: Oh my God. <u>This can't be true. No, no.</u> (He covers his eyes.) Oh my God.

(He quiets down for five seconds.)

A: Would you wanna talk to her family tonight?

(He starts crying again and hits his legs a couple of times. No answer. Then he is quiet again for a few seconds. Then he starts again...) <u>No, no, no.</u>

1:29 a.m. – Answer: Why? (He asks this question out loud for the first time.)

A: Everything that I've heard says that this has been a horrible accident.

(Man rubs his head and continues to cry.)

Answer: Oh my God. <u>Can't be true.</u> (He takes some deep breaths and is quiet for a few seconds.) <u>This can't be true.</u> (He shakes his head. He rubs his head. He places his hands over his eyes for several seconds.) <u>Can't be true. It can't be true.</u> (He folds his hands in grief and leans back.)

1:30 a.m. – A: The first thing to do is just get through the next hour.

Answer: Have to get myself together. First thing.

(It is quiet for 30 seconds.)

A: Do you feel like you did everything you could tonight?

(He is very quiet. Then he turns to look at me for the first time.)

Answer: What?!

A: Do you feel like you did everything you could tonight for her?

Answer: Yes. (A few heavy sighs.) … I'm so sorry. I'm so sorry, … all because of a stupid argument. (He places his hands over his eyes; then folds his hands in front of his nose.)

A: Did you say she was being stubborn?

(He doesn't answer the question.)

1:31 a.m. – Answer: You know, we buried my little granddaughter today.

A: (You can see a mild look of shock on my face, my mouth drops) You say you buried your granddaughter?

Answer: It was my granddaughter's little daughter.

A: Really? What happened?

1:32 a.m. – Answer: She died.

A: Was she sick?

Answer: No. She lived only about five minutes [after birth].

A: Oh, you guys had a funeral for her today?

Answer: Yes. They couldn't come up with the money…so I paid for the funeral.

(A few seconds of silence.)

Answer: I've been living with her for five years.

A: Mm-hmm [yes].

Answer: Separated from my other wife. And her health ain't that good. So I told her...so I went ahead and got her insurance...whatever you call it. Insurance?

A: Mm-hmm [yes]. Health insurance?

Answer: Pre-paid insurance or whatever you call it.

A: Mm-hmm. Makes sense.

Answer: She and I got to arguing about that. (He takes a few big breaths.)

A: Like, you shouldn't have done that?

Answer: Yeah, like I shouldn't have done that.

1:33 a.m. – A: But you were just trying to help her out?

Answer: Well, somebody's got to bury her—my ex-wife.

A: Mm-hmm.

Answer: She and I got to arguing. She said, "Well, how come you buy her insurance and you can't buy me insurance?" I said, "But you got all [my] benefits and everything else from me."

A: So, she felt jealous?

Answer: All my retirement. It's all in her name. If something happened to me, she would be... [his words fade out]. She and I got to arguing about that, and then she got out. ... Oh my God. <u>I can't believe this. I can't believe this. It didn't happen...it didn't happen.</u>

1:34 a.m. – Answer: (to the police officer in the front seat) Can I go, sir, please?

117

O: We gotta get someone to come and take your statement, okay? You see one of these gentlemen out here taking photos? They gotta do things in a certain order before they talk to you. Okay? They are trying to make it fast and efficient. But the seriousness of the situation means they got to do things in a certain order. All right?

(All is quiet for a few seconds.)

1:35 a.m. – Answer: <u>I can't believe this, no.</u>

O: I promise, you won't be here longer than you have to be. Okay?

(Quiet again for a few seconds.)

Answer: Did they pick up everything? (The man starts to cry again.)

O: Sir?

Answer: Did they pick up everything?

O: They are gonna do that here in a little bit. They have to take pictures of everything first.

Answer: I don't know if she had her purse with her or not. Oh my God. <u>I can't believe this is true.</u> Oh my God, <u>no.</u>

1:36 a.m. – A: I don't want you to have to be home alone tonight. Are you gonna be staying by yourself?

(The man does not answer. He continues to stare out the window as he has been doing much of the time. He is quiet for about 45 seconds.)

A: Sounds like they may want to talk to you in an office instead of in the back of a police car.

1:37 a.m. – Answer: I just want to go home. I need to go notify her family. ... God, <u>I can't believe this is true, I can't believe this is true. I can't...</u>

A: Would you like me to be there while you do that? To help you tell them about it?

Answer: No…I can tell them. (The man is sobbing more quietly now.)

Answer: Come on, just let me go home. <u>I can't believe this is true. I can't believe she died.</u>

1:38 a.m. – A: Yeah, it sounds like it happened awfully quick.

Answer: (wiping his face) <u>I can't believe this. Can't believe this.</u> (He beats his fists into his legs.) … I wanna go home. … I wanna go home. … I wanna go home. (Sobs start again.) Oh my God, I wanna go home. (He is shaking his head back and forth.)

* * *

At 1:39 a.m., the officer looks in the car and says, "Andy, you can step out of the car now," and then he says to the grieving gentleman, "I'm gonna take you to the police department now."
"Why?" the man asks.
"We've got to get a statement from you. Then you can go home. Nothing will happen with your truck. The police will make sure of that."
"Can I just take my truck home now?"
"No, sir, you can't."
Then the video and the audio are turned off.
I also travel to the police department to be available, if needed.
Eventually, the incident was determined to be an accident, and no one was charged.

* * *

It was difficult to sit with him in such intense grief, but being there was better than him being alone. In the majority of situations, immediately after witnessing or hearing of a personal tragic circumstance, a victim will not want to talk about the situation fully, nor might they give detailed answers, simply because they are not able to. In any case, regardless of what they can or cannot say or do, the job of a Victim Services Crisis counselor is to be there, consoling and guiding that person through those first dark moments. The next chapter addresses more specifically the help we provide and how we do that job.

CHAPTER EIGHT
BRINGING ORDER TO THE CHAOS

"Blessed are the peacemakers, for they will be called children of God."

—Matthew 5:9 (NIV)

As I have worked as a crisis counselor and hostage negotiator, I've kept in mind the question, "What is expected of me?" I've also considered how I can best help any individual or family as they fight their way through the first dark moments and emotional fallout from a personal calamity.

When I show up at the scene of a crisis or in someone's home in response to an emergency call, my personal style and preference is to not insert myself or to say a whole lot. As a stranger trying to help someone grieving, that type of initial interaction feels intrusive to me. Rather, after being introduced by an officer or introducing myself, I usually sense God's leadings, such as, "Go sit next to that person so that they're not alone. I want you to represent me and show them that I see what's happening right now and that I care about them."

And to sit there or stand nearby, quietly and respectfully, might be my only job.

Often, though, I will also provide some basic support and comfort, involving what I consider to be simple tasks but which seem to be most significant for those suffering. Some professional counselors call it "psychological first aid" (PFA). I'm not there to provide therapy or to make everything better immediately. But rather, as sensibly as I can, I try to provide a few good *antidotes* to what can be construed as the *toxins* of a crisis.[18]

1. **The Toxin**—*Anxiety*, **The Antidote**—*Calm*

During most any personal catastrophe, the anxiety level of the individual(s) affected is almost always amplified. Thus, my first responsibility is to exhibit a calm and peaceful presence, offering an authentic concern and a desire to help. This is never a time to try to be something that I'm not, and most people, even when stressed, can usually see right through that type of phony posture. I maintain a quiet, controlled demeanor to help calm the victim, speaking slowly and clearly in order to help bring some peace.

Have you ever been around someone who is freaking out and another person yells, "Calm down!"? That scenario is the opposite of what I'm saying here. Screaming at someone who is experiencing a traumatic situation is not helpful. "It's their emergency, not my emergency" is an EMS phrase that I think of often. I am of little help to someone else if I'm upset as well. Moreover, the more difficult time they are having, the more calm and stable I need to be.

I want my presence and words to reflect *genuine* empathy, concern, understanding, and patience—especially patience. Most victims cannot completely grasp the crisis that has just occurred, and they need someone nearby who can offer them the space and as much time as possible to work through their emotions as well as consider the actions and decisions they will soon have to make.

---

18 For more about crisis intervention, I recommend Richard James and Burt Gilliland, *Crisis Intervention Strategies*, Brooks/Cole, 2013.

2. **The Toxin**—*Chaos,* **The Antidote**—*Safety and Structure*

All members of our Victim Services Crisis Team (VSCT) are taught to make assessments as quickly as they can upon first arriving at the scene of a crisis, with regard to all factors that might be contributing to the chaos—the environment, the mood of all people involved or in the area, the unhelpfulness of well-intentioned family or friends, the possibility of any weapons or other potentially dangerous objects nearby; and likewise, be attentive to doorways and windows providing an exit, as well as any other safe areas where a victim can be moved in order to minimize any physical and/or psychological dangers. We may need to divide people up and talk with them separately. We also must determine if the additional help of a police officer or an EMT is needed.

People whose world has just been turned upside down by an unforeseeable trauma may find it very hard to talk and/or make decisions. Hence, crisis counselors figuratively, and may literally, hold their hand and say, "You're safe now. This is what I'm going to do to help you get through the next hour. And this is what I need you to do." We lay out the order of what will happen next, with regard to any police investigation or perhaps the involvement of a medical examiner and mortuary service. We also may need to explain the decisions an individual or family will need to make and can give them some advice and point out their options.

Meanwhile, and often before a victim is able to make any decisions, a counselor will continue to exercise patience and understanding while a victim moves back and forth from an emotional to a cognitive state, as we discussed in the last chapter. During this time, it is extremely important for a counselor to speak slowly, continually offer words of comfort, repeat the facts clearly but with empathy, and repeat questions as many times as necessary. A counselor will also paraphrase the victim's answer so he is sure that he clearly understands what the victim is saying. Usually, the use of open-ended questions, which require more thought and detailed answers from the victim, is more productive than using closed-ended questions, which merely ask for a "yes" or "no" answer.

3. **The Toxin**—*Dysfunctional Emotions,* **The Antidote**—*Rational/Logical Thinking*

It is normal for people to become very emotional during a crisis—some become quite distraught, others angry, some very quiet, and others hysterical. But no matter what emotion they exhibit, their memory will probably be affected. Again, it is important that someone be there to help them rationally process what has just happened. When things get really hot, chaotic, and disruptive, it's easy to think things that aren't accurate and might be harmful. At these times, I offer the truth clearly, sometimes even in a confrontational manner.

For example, in the case of a driver accidentally hitting and killing a drunken pedestrian who was walking in the middle of the road at nighttime, I don't know how many times I've heard some derivative of "I killed them." or "It's my fault." Even though it is clear to everyone involved and all emergency personnel who respond to the scene that it was an accident, some drivers still insist on taking on this false responsibility.

In cases where these drivers inappropriately blame themselves, I am tempted to ask questions such as, "Did you see the pedestrian and then speed up on purpose? Did you accelerate and aim for him? Did you try to hit him?" This is my definition of trying to kill a person with a vehicle. And most every time, if not always, the answer would be, "No, of course I didn't try to hit him on purpose." What I usually ask is something like, "What makes you think this is your fault?" and then try to walk people through how irrational their answer might be. I also often offer a clear alternative as well as the truth. If the driver, however, continues to insist on believing that he is responsible for killing someone, there is not much more I can do. A few times, I've laid out for a person the harm associated with continuing to believe what they believe. Meanwhile, he becomes a strong candidate for post-traumatic stress disorder (PTSD). It's not the event that causes PTSD symptoms, but rather the individual's interpretation and the meaning they give that event.

On other occasions, I will show up at the scene of a suicide and will hear loved ones struggle and make statements such as, "I had no idea they were depressed. But…I should have known," or "I think I could have stopped it," indicating a level of responsibility for this person's death.

I often reply, "If you had known that this person was going to commit suicide today, what would you have done?" And they will answer something like, "I would have begged them to stop," or "I would have called the police," or "I would have been there to make sure they didn't harm themselves." Then I say, "So, had you known, you would have done something differently?"

"Yes."

"You would have stopped it?"

"Yes."

Sometimes, this logical sequence of questions helps; at other times, people just continue to beat themselves up.

When an individual takes on too much blame, he or she is actually confessing that they think they are more powerful than they truly are. In the cases above, these people couldn't have stopped the accident or the suicide. They weren't that powerful. Had they been given that power or knowledge, they would have stopped it. Part of my job is to help them understand and accept that difficult truth in a time of crisis.

Even when people say, "I knew she was depressed, but I didn't know what to do" or "I feel so bad that I didn't take him more seriously—I didn't think he would do it," I'll ask them, "What did you see that indicated this person was going to kill themselves?" Almost always, the people will retract their initial statement and say, "But I didn't know [this], and I didn't know [that]." And I will continue to listen as they wrestle back and forth, and then attempt to help them figure this out. They may struggle for a few minutes, days, weeks, or even years. But for those few hours that I spend with them, I do what I can to help them land in a place of "I can't hold myself responsible for how this turned out."

In other crisis situations, I will hear a woman blame herself for the crime of rape that has been committed against her, especially if she thinks she will have a difficult time convincing others to believe her, if she bears no physical marks, or if she is the victim of a "date rape." She feels responsible because she chose to get into a car with a guy, or she had too much to drink, or she wore seductive clothing, or was told that she "asked for it." That's all nonsense.

Unfortunately, though, many of those circumstances make it that much harder for her to report, and practically speaking, much harder for the judicial system to convict. My role, again, is to help the victim sort through what has just happened. As a counselor, this takes a lot of care and sophistication. Usually, in these cases where a woman feels some sort of responsibility, she will not reveal the perpetrator. Whatever her decision, though, my job is to help her cope and begin to heal. Every once in a while I can help her appropriately assign the blame for what has happened. Even more rarely, I get to help her walk through forgiveness.

4. **The Toxin**—*Tension and Frustration,* **The Antidote**—*Catharsis*

As a crisis counselor, not only am I responsible for moving victims to a physical place where they feel safe but I also provide an atmosphere where they feel comfortable enough to express the tension and frustration they are experiencing. They should be allowed to purge or vent any pent-up emotions in a safe environment.

This is the time that I need to *listen* and not be distracted by my own thoughts or worries. This is not the time for me to concentrate on how I am performing as a counselor or how my own past experiences relate to what the victim is going through at present. At the scene of a crisis, the focus is on the victim.

Listening is a tough skill, and I've found that paraphrasing what the victims say helps me to pay attention and helps them process their thoughts and feelings. When someone describes where they found their son lying in a pool of blood, or how they felt when they heard that their mother died, I must concentrate on what this means for them—not think of something from my own past. That type of reflection is selfish.

After my responsibilities with the victims have been completed and I return home, I can then reflect on my own life and personal crises and consider how I might have handled this particular situation differently and how I might do better the next time.

Sometimes during the release of emotions, tension or frustration, it has seemed that these emotions became directed at me. For instance, when it seems that someone is now angry with me, I like to check in with the person in the moment and ask them about it directly. Similarly, it's a good practice to not take anything personally, even if it is directed at me. Rather, working through the thoughts and emotions, even if I've somehow become part of the problem, seems the best way to assist people. I'll give an example of this at the end of the chapter.

5. **The Toxin**—*Loss of Control,* **The Antidote**—*Information* **and** *Truth*

In the previous chapter, I discussed the reaction of the man who saw his wife accidentally hit and killed by a car. Many people like him say, "No, no, no. This can't be happening. It can't be true." And they might say these words over and over again. They are not saying, "This is a lie." Nor are they saying to me, "You're lying; I don't believe you." They *are* saying, "I can't handle this right now."

Part of my job then is to help them adjust to reality. I say clearly, compassionately, and at the right time, "This is reality. I know it is terrible. But this *is* what happened."

The reality might be, "I'm sorry to tell you this, but your loved one drowned earlier today at the lake and is not coming home." For some people, this sounds cruel. Indeed, the truth may be awful, but hiding or denying or dancing around the truth would be worse.

"He shot himself…in the head…on the back porch." "Your dad killed your mom … then he killed himself." "Your daughter was out with some friends and was killed in a car accident at 2:00 a.m." When I present such disheartening news, I keep in mind that this information is not something that someone can quickly adjust to. Therefore, I might need to repeat the facts a few more times until they can begin to comprehend this new reality.

However, some people still might not be able to grasp the truth. At that point, I can't become uptight or irritated. Rather, I must exercise compassion and give them as much time as they need to process what has actually happened.

When a child is devastated by the death of his pet dog, the same principle applies. We should respect his grief, but still do what is necessary to help him work through his denial and to slowly come to terms with the truth. Likewise, in cases as difficult as a sexual assault, we allow that woman or man as long as they need. In one of my counseling cases, I met with a woman for four one-hour sessions within a month before she could get to the place where she could say, "I was raped."

It's not fun to be the guy to help a girl say and articulate, "I was raped." But I've determined that to help people, those types of uncomfortable situations are part of the deal. To heal, people have to come to terms with what actually happened. That healing cannot begin until the victim can admit that a crime was committed against them, or that an accident happened, or that a loved one has died. And sometimes, it can take a while to do that.

Whether or not a person begins to accept reality at the scene of a crisis, my job is also to give them information regarding what to expect and what they might want to do next.

Sometimes, people express their desire to view a loved one's body before the mortuary service takes them away. When I hear such a request, I advise, "I think it's better to remember them as they were, not as they are now." But for some people, the sight of their loved one, no matter what he or she looks like, actually benefits them. Perhaps they are not able to make sense of the situation until they view the body, or they simply need to say "good-bye," or perhaps they want to proclaim their love one more time. Usually, though, I feel that the majority of people are better off remembering their loved one as they were.

All too soon, many people, even while they are distraught and grieving, must also deal with a medical examiner, mortuary service, and funeral home. Occasionally, some people will begin to talk about a funeral or memorial service and ask for my guidance in this area as well.

My advice is to be very careful of whom you allow to speak at this solemn occasion. Many inappropriate comments have been made at funerals by people who wanted to talk more about themselves than about the deceased. I would label that as self-centered. And the last place you want a self-centered person is at a service honoring and remembering your loved one.

Likewise, some teenagers are too immature to speak at a funeral and don't understand the implications of sharing childish stories that they think are humorous or praiseworthy, but actually devastates or embarrasses the parents and family.

And I'll add that I don't understand the need for a sermon of hellfire and brimstone, or a preacher calling people to baptism, etc. We can trust that people are already taking stock of their own lives, asking God all kinds of questions, and seeking Him for answers. My recommendation is to ask only those people who personally knew the deceased to participate in the service, and to include pictures, thoughts, music, other personal memorabilia—whatever makes the service meaningful—whether it is something traditional or not.

6. **The Toxin**—*Alienation/Disconnection*, **The Antidote**—*Social Support*

Immediately after a crisis occurs, I, as a counselor, cannot, nor do I plan to, "save the day." This is never a time for a MHP to go in and show everyone else how important they think they are. No one can quickly fix or correct the situation. When someone experiences a travesty—for example, the loss of an infant—no one can make that right in an hour.

As I previously mentioned, our counselors show up in an emergency to give basic aid and support—to communicate that we care about the people suffering and assure them that help is available. In addition, our VSCT members are also educated about several agencies and organizations that provide various types of social support and are able to refer victims according to their needs.

When a tragedy—an *abnormal* event—occurs, victims may erroneously think, *I'm the only one who has ever had to live through something like this*. And for that moment, right then and there, at that location, and with the people involved, they are the *only* person experiencing such an ordeal. But the whole truth is, they are not alone, and multitudes of people have dealt with suffering. Thus, it is important to offer that information and provide an opportunity for them to connect with people who have lived through similar experiences.

Our crisis counselors help the victim identify what type of help they might need, available resources, and social and situational supports (e.g., agencies, pastoral care, family, friends, crisis worker/counselor, social worker, or people known to the victim who might care about what happens to them). We can also help the victim(s) form a plan for the next few days—a plan that emphasizes their independence, control, and self-care. And so we discuss coping mechanisms they might want to try, such as exercise, meditation, expression, sports, prayer, and writing.

7. **The Toxin**—*Helplessness and Fear*, **The Antidote**—*Peace and Trust*

Even while people are struggling with denial and shock, grief and fear, some will begin to ask difficult "why" questions. And when someone asks why, they are asking something bigger than themselves for an answer. Sometimes, a person will be open to the answers. On other occasions, he or she is not yet ready, so we need to focus on more immediate needs and problems. Common questions I hear are along the lines of, "How am I going to live without her? Why did this happen? What do I do now?"

Again, my job is to help them explore the answers they may already have, but are harder to see because of the situation and stress, and possibly give them other options to consider. I'm also a man of faith, so in the back of my mind are some questions for God that they may want to ask Him, and in turn, may bring peace. Some of these questions they might ask are: "God, what are You doing here?" "What is Your will or purpose here?" "Where were You when this happened?" or "Where am I to go from here?" There are times when I encourage the people I'm talking with to ask and seek answers to these questions. I also encourage peace, trust, and patience as they do, especially because so much is going on and needs to be sorted through. But, there are also times when the answers to these questions begin to emerge relatively quickly, and I love watching people gain peace, faith, trust, and comfort from being able to see where God is or where He was during times of crisis and calamity. And of course, as is appropriate and beneficial for the person I'm talking to, I will also offer (usually gently, sometimes clearly) what I see for them to consider.

* * *

Throughout the years, I've made a sincere effort to provide the previously listed antidotes, and yet sometimes, something still goes wrong. I recall that in one case I was kicked out of a home.

The police called me at about 3:00 a.m. and requested my help at a residence where a high school student had hung and killed himself in his bedroom.

When I showed up at the family's home, a lieutenant met me in the front yard and updated me with regard to the facts of the situation. While he was talking, he said, "…and I told the family that Dr. Young will be coming over. He's a professor over at the university and a counselor…and Dr. Young will do this…and Dr. Young will be able to help you with that…."

Obvious to me was that he had laid on the "Dr. Young" stuff pretty thick (whereas, at most scenes, I'm known as "Andy"). In any case, after the officer finished giving the update, I proceeded inside the home, where I sat with the mother, the father, and the brother of the victim.

As was my usual manner, I sat down and remained quiet for a while to see if anyone felt up to discussing what had happened. Soon, the mother started to talk.

"We went to bed. I thought everything was fine. I didn't know anything was going on with him."

The father likewise spoke up, "I heard his music playing about 1:00 a.m. so I went to his room to see what was goin' on. And when I opened the door, I found him hanging there."

The mom then mentioned that she knew he was a little depressed but thought it was just normal teenage stuff.

"So…this was just kind of a normal type of depression? You didn't expect anything?" I paraphrased.

Suddenly, the dad became angry. He jumped to his feet and shouted, "What kind of doctor are you, asking some question like that?" And he proceeded to climb my tree.

Meanwhile, the mother and brother attempted to intervene, saying to the dad, "Calm down. He's just here to help. This shouldn't be a problem."

Eventually, the dad sat back down, and the mom started to talk again.

I then repeated a few phrases she said and clarified a few of her comments.

And all of sudden, the dad lit up once more, and this time, he started to pace around behind me.

"What kind of doctor asks that kind of question?"

Again, the mom and the son tried to calm him down.

In another moment, everyone stopped talking, and a big, awkward silence filled the room. I tried not to make eye contact with the officer there in the room with us.

Sincerely hoping to improve this situation, I slowly turned to the dad and said, "I apologize. I really didn't mean to offend you."

But evidently, that wasn't the right approach either, because instantly, the dad twisted off again, with the mom and brother trying to smooth things over.

At this point, I thought it best that I see about an exit and asked, "Would you like me to leave?"

"Yeah, I want you to leave!" he demanded, while the mom interjected, "No, no, no…I think he should stay."

I felt in this case I should honor the father's wishes. So I said, "Good night," and walked out to the car, thanking God I could get home at a reasonable time and get back to bed.

But I took only a few more steps when I decided that I just couldn't leave because I knew what was coming next—the ME and mortuary service would soon be there—and I felt I should stick around to help the family with this process and with the likely questions. Even so, at that moment, I didn't want to go back inside the house. So…I stood out in the cold, on the front porch.

In the meantime, a friend of the family came by, and soon, the ME also arrived.

"What are you doing out here?" the familiar face from the ME's office asked when she saw me standing there.

"Well…I just got kicked out."

"What?"

"Yeah, I just got kicked out. The dad wants nothing to do with me."

She raised her eyebrows and her eyes got big, revealing her own apprehension about going inside. But inside she went.

A few minutes later, an officer came out of the house. Folding his arms and with an amused look on his face, he said, "So what did you do wrong?"

"Man, I have no idea. I pretty much just paraphrased what his wife was saying, and he just went up one side of me and down the other." The officer shrugged and went back inside.

I ended up standing on that front porch for about 45 minutes. The ME and the mortuary service both came and went, and eventually, the lieutenant who introduced me came out of the house and also asked me what the problem was.

So I told him the same story. Then he went back in the house and came back out again a bit later.

"Okay, Andy, I know what happened."

"You do? Because *I* don't know what happened."

"I talked to the friend about how the father reacted to you, and the friend said, 'Oh, I know why he went off. His wife had an affair with a doctor, so obviously, he had a problem with your counselor being a doctor."

"Well, there you go. Ninety-nine calls out of 100, I never learn why people do or say the things they do. But this time, I understood what I did to set this man off. Good thing I didn't take any of that personally."

"No worries, Andy," the lieutenant smiled. "We'll make sure we always introduce you as 'the Doc' from now on."

CHAPTER NINE
VIOLENCE IN THE HOME

"I need someone to come right away…my daughter's holding my wife at gunpoint!"

Shortly after this 911 call came in, I was contacted by the police and reported to a serious domestic situation. While a woman was threatening to shoot her elderly mother, her father had escaped from the house and was waiting outside.

Minutes later, when I pulled up near the designated location, I saw that two patrol cars were already sitting directly in front of the residence. Kneeling behind the vehicles were two officers with weapons drawn and eyes fixed on the house. A SWAT callout had been initiated, and other officers were taking control of the street. Likewise, the command unit was en route and would be set up around the corner, about half a block away.

Meanwhile, I called out on the radio, "I'm 10-23," notifying Dispatch that I was at the scene; for the time being, I knew it best to stay in my car.

Very soon, though, one of the officers came back across the radio, saying, "Andy, we need you at the ambulance on the west side of the house."

"Okay," I responded, "I'm sitting on the east side."

"Stand by," he instructed. "We're coming to get you."

By the time I grabbed my helmet, vest and some other gear, an officer (also with his rifle drawn) approached my car window.

"Andy, I'm here to take you to see the man who placed the call. And since we're going right past the house where his daughter his holding his wife hostage, I need you to walk on the other side of me and stay real close."

Straightaway, I got out of the car, and as he began to step sideways down the street with his rifle pointed toward the house, I made very sure he was always between me and whoever it was that might want to make me a target.

Within another minute, we made it safely to the ambulance, where the officer introduced me to the paramedics as well as to an elderly gentleman who was sitting on the back of the ambulance and was obviously traumatized.

As I began to talk with him and ask several questions, he repeated more than a few times that his daughter had taken his wife hostage at gunpoint and was now holding her in one of the bedrooms. Dealing with an elderly individual can sometimes be challenging. A person up in years might not be able to move or talk as fast as we would like, and for some people, this can be trying. Yet knowing that I needed to acquire as much information as quickly as possible while also understanding it would be counterproductive if this man became even more upset, I simply exercised a little more patience, a calm tone, and understanding. The extra effort paid off, and within a short time, the other negotiator who joined me and I had names and phone numbers of his family members (including the information of a grown son and daughter). Other negotiators then spread out in all directions to start making calls, hopefully to chase down any information that might help us deal with this situation and the daughter holding the mother inside.

Very soon, in fact within about 15 minutes, I was pulled away from the gentleman at the ambulance and presented with a number of enlightening facts:

First, we discovered that his wife was deceased. She had died five years prior.

Second, we learned that the daughter who was supposedly inside the house, actually lived in Arkansas. Her address and phone number were obtained, and she was likewise given a call.

Third, we found out this man actually lived alone.

Fourth, we were told that four years ago, he had placed an emergency call and described a similar scenario. At that time, EMS personnel discovered early on that such an emergency did not exist; consequently, the man's request for help hadn't risen to the response level of this occasion.

Fifth, this elderly man had been diagnosed with Parkinson's disease some years ago.

Talking with officers and various family members that day, I learned that a few side effects of certain medications for Parkinson's disease often can include confusion, hallucinations, and delusions, especially if a person suddenly stops and then starts taking his medication again. In other words, a person may become a little psychotic and lose touch with reality. Naturally, during discussions that day, we wondered if this man had recently stopped and started taking the medication again.

In the meantime, I also took a few moments to contact the state mental health agency to see if or how they should get involved. As we continued to gather all the information, SWAT remained in place, and at some point, I remember one of the rifle teams positioned on the roof of a house across the street notified Command that local observers were coming too close in order to take pictures (a common ramification of these events).

Ultimately, in light of all the facts we were able to gather, the police determined that most likely there was no threat within this man's residence, yet they were not about to foolishly take any chances. Assuming that someone or something dangerous might still be inside, the SWAT commander decided to send in a robot along with a SWAT contingent to inspect the target bedroom as well as search all other areas of the house. Some negotiators joined them inside to call out to the bedroom indicated by the man with whom we'd been talking.

A short time later, police confirmed that no one was in the bedroom or in any other part of the residence. Upon this substantiation, I walked over to the gentleman still sitting on the back of the ambulance, and took a few minutes to outline as clearly as I could what we had learned throughout the day.

"From what I understand, sir," I said as gently as I could, "your wife died five years ago."

He simply nodded, and I could see the bewilderment, yet at the same time, understanding in his eyes.

"And from what I've been hearing today, the daughter you mentioned—the one who you thought might be in the house…well…she lives in Arkansas."

Again, he silently nodded his head.

As he continued to listen, I addressed all the facts, as I knew them. By and by, when I finished giving him the report, he said with some resignation, "It must be that damn medication again."

"Yes sir. It seems so," I replied. "We'd like to help you. So, we brought your family here. My advice is to get them to take you to see your doctor and get this worked out." Accordingly, the family members, who were present, were likewise very helpful and willing to take care of him.

At this time, all SWAT and other EMS personnel who had been prepared to react to a serious case of domestic violence, began to pack up instead. The amateur photographers walked away somewhat disappointed. The police negotiators and crisis team members congratulated each other on another good training exercise.

* * *

In the year 2014, the Lubbock Police Department as well as our Victim Services Crisis Team responded to many calls relating to domestic disputes, as well as to requests for help that involved more severe domestic abuse and violence. Specifically, the department's

Violence in the Home

Crime Report,[19] for the period 1/1/2014—12/31/2014, indicates that the police department dealt with 124 reports of "family offenses"; yet many others of the 38,861 crimes reported that year, such as the ones listed below, did or probably involved domestic-related or family issues as well:

- Child abuse – 83 reports
- Child neglect/abandonment, nonsupport – 33 reports
- Harassment – 590 reports
- Indecency with a child – 60 reports
- Juvenile curfew violation – 16 reports
- Missing person/adult, juveniles – 68 reports
- Rape – 123 reports
- Runaway/juvenile – 413 reports
- Stalking – 49 reports
- Statutory rape – 15 reports
- Stolen vehicle/civil matters – 201 reports
- Truancy – 11 reports
- Violation of protective order – 69 reports

Considering that even a small percentage of the calls listed above dealt with family disputes, abuse, or violence, it's no wonder the Victim Services Crisis Team was first founded based on the need for help with domestic-related incidents.

I remember one callout during the fall of 2008. At 9:50 on a Friday morning, a report was received that a suicidal man and his wife were fighting, at which time the man allegedly grabbed a pistol and shot it into the ceiling. When police arrived at the residence, the wife met

---

19   For a complete list of all crime reports for the year 2014, please see the document, "Crimes for Lubbock, Texas," Lubbock Police Department, 01/01/2014—12/31/2014; pp. 1-3.

them outside and stated that her husband was inside the residence and had access to guns.

During the next three hours, their entire neighborhood block was stacked full of police cars, the SWAT team, the command unit, and a support truck. I likewise reported to the scene and met with other negotiators, while additional Crisis Team members showed up to meet with members of the family, including the wife, the mother, and the father of the subject.

About an hour into the call, one of the police negotiators was able to contact the armed man inside who said he was calm and lying down. After that conversation, however, the subject never answered his phone. Then, within the next half hour, the media showed up.

Throughout the entire ordeal, I continued to talk with the wife, the parents, and other relatives; and from almost the very beginning of the callout, the entire family saw no need for, nor did they think the situation warranted this much intervention or response. For a couple hours, I kept receiving the same information and hearing the same type of comments: "Everyone just needs to go home." "This has happened before—he's probably sleeping, and all this fuss is unnecessary." "Please—all these cops just need to go away." "He'll sober up and probably not remember anything." Even the wife said, "He'll be fine, and I can just go to my parents' house until he sleeps this off."

In support of the family, I reported to the command post and informed one of the assistant chiefs of their request. Discussions ensued, and after a while, the assistant chief looked at some of his subordinates and said, "Well, should this guy be arrested, and if so, for what?"

The consensus was: absolutely nothing of substance.

Every officer there understood that discharge of a firearm within the city limits was not worth kicking in the door or starting a firefight. The guy inside had every right to tear up his own house. Moreover, we hadn't heard from him for at least two hours—proof to his family that he was most likely sleeping off a drunken stupor and not aware of the commotion he had created.

Ultimately, the assistant chief agreed we should go about facilitating the family's wishes, even though it felt kind of awkward to call off a mass of police and SWAT vehicles while the "whole world" was watching. At the same time, a few other negotiators and I talked with the family about how they should proceed in the next few hours and days to ensure their own safety, and to definitely call us if anything changed or went bad. In this case, the family turned out to be right. When I called to follow up the next day, they confirmed that everything seemed to be okay. For another two or three days, the cops kept an eye on their residence until it was determined no further assistance was needed.

I've dealt with many other families, however, and especially women, who haven't been quite this fortunate. What may have begun as just an argument or loud yelling, all of a sudden spun out of control and turned violent—even deadly.

* * *

Not long after I'd started volunteering as a crisis counselor, I was called to Covenant Hospital to meet with a woman whose husband had assaulted her. But before he did, he gave her an idea of how much pain he was about to inflict. "If I'm gonna go to jail for kicking your ass," he spouted, "I'm gonna make it worth the trip." Then with a pair of steel-toed boots, he kicked, and hammered, and pounded all parts of her body—especially her head and face.

That evening, I was called as a crisis counselor for the obvious reason—to help, comfort, and talk with a victim of domestic abuse. I soon learned, though, that I was contacted for two other reasons as well. First—just after the ambulance brought her in, this woman told me that she was alone—all alone—and that she had no one else to call. Consequently, one of the officers, feeling much compassion, expressed his desire that I stay as long as possible with her. Moreover, because this officer was highly motivated to go find the bad guy and throw him in jail for what he had done, my presence would ensure he could get to that task all the faster. Second—because the officers were extremely busy that evening, they needed someone to take pictures of this woman's horrible bruises and deep, ugly gashes, as she lay still, secured to a backboard on a hospital bed.

As I went about handling my extra responsibilities, I continued to talk with this woman and discussed much of what I, as well as other Crisis Team counselors, have learned in training with regard to dealing with domestic abuse victims as well as the perpetrators.

In fact, in our line of work, it is conducive to understand as much about the abusive man's common psychological factors as it is to be familiar with those mental and emotional traits of the battered woman. Please note: I understand that a person who is abusive is not always a *man*. Likewise, a person described as battered is not always a *woman*. However, in this text, to describe the characteristics of both types of people, we'll use "man" as the abusive party and "woman" as the abused.

The man who is abusive usually demonstrates excessive dependency and possessiveness over the woman whom he is abusing, but he'll probably deny it. In many cases, this man does not possess good communication skills, and he is often unable to express any emotion except anger. He is demanding and aggressive, cruel and hostile. He sets rigid boundaries and unrealistic expectations of his female partner. At the same time, he lacks self-control and is impulsive, and is often an alcoholic or a drug abuser. Very likely, he was abused himself as a child. However, he minimizes any family problems, particularly the battering at present, insisting that his actions are "not that bad," and will even deny the abuse. He is likewise a jealous person, suffers from depression, and belittles himself.

The battered woman also lacks self-esteem and has little or no confidence in herself. And like her abuser, she often does not possess good communication skills. Different from her abuser, however, who is aggressive and demanding, she usually feels she has little control of the situation. Often, she has a history of being abused and has learned to hide her physical and emotional wounds. In many cases, an abused woman lacks any type of resources—personal, physical, educational, or financial; therefore, she is dependent. She considers stereotypical sexual roles to be the truth, and most likely, she is unable to differentiate between sex and love. Or to put it another way, she believes that love is manifested through intense sexual acts.

When our Crisis Team members learn how to help the police provide some type of intervention, we are instructed to always reassure the woman that we believe her reports of being battered. At first contact, we do what we can, but our intervention is able to accomplish only so much protection. We cannot make decisions that can be made only by the victim. No matter how bad the situation appears, the victim has to decide for herself when she is ready to take action and must take steps to leave the abusive environment. We cannot insist that a battered woman move any faster than she is willing to go; we cannot "fix" the situation for her. Only she can set the pace, and the statistics indicate that it will take her about five times of leaving him and then returning before she is able to leave him and not go back.

It's difficult to witness and often hard to accept that many times an abused victim is afraid of independence. Up until this point, she probably hasn't experienced self-sufficiency to any degree, and even with assistance, there is a great risk she will fall back into a dependent state—upon the abuser; or if she leaves the abusive situation, she may somehow try to shift her responsibilities onto others, including family members, the police, or a counselor.

In order to truly help herself, she needs to realize that others cannot solve her problems; rather, she must take responsibility for herself. This can be a long process, though. It can be easy for a crisis worker, or anyone else who wants to help, to become overly involved and attempt to "fix" the problem. Sometimes, each of us may need to be reminded of our boundaries and stick to offering alternatives.

First and foremost, the most important way to help is to *actively listen*. It is imperative that the victim realizes how much the crisis worker understands and accepts the situation without being judgmental.

Second, the VSCT members are trained to be supportive because many battered women feel that they lack social support and understanding. Therefore, one of our primary responsibilities is to make sure these women know that someone cares—someone who will also allow them to vent. When battered victims open up, they tend to express many feelings—feelings of fear, hurt, depression, and guilt. Beneath these emotions often lies a volatile and unexpressed anger. We, as friends and counselors, empathize and allow time for an abused woman to express these feelings. We learn to be sensitive and understanding, yet again, without trying to take over the woman's responsibilities.

Third, our team members facilitate movement for the individual or family victims. At this point, workers might have to deal with the victim's sense of dependency, ambivalence, and depression, which can be trying, at times, and thus require patience. It's a hard, hard thing for many women to leave a family home, even a dangerous and abusive one. We may define this as "learned helplessness." But whatever anyone chooses to call it, a crisis worker is there to reinforce the victim's attempts at rational decision-making and doing what is best for her and her family. Even the abuser can benefit from her making changes and communicating through her behavior that the abuser's behavior cannot continue. By using open-ended questions, restating what the victim has said, and reflecting the woman's emotions, the crisis worker can point out and help eliminate the victim's faulty thinking and illogical perceptions of the event and begin to encourage movement.

Fourth, our team remains constantly aware of the woman's safety. Specifically, we immediately determine how critical the situation is and assess any imminent danger. Then we must answer questions such as: What is the safest and quickest way to get out of the house? Does the victim need shelter for herself and her children? Does anyone require medical attention? Then we take appropriate action.

Fifth, we advocate for the victim. An abused woman often has little knowledge of alternatives and of the judicial system, so introducing them to various resources and providing those resources is most helpful.

Our team members also learn the purpose of an Emergency Protective Order (EPO), a tool that can be used for or on behalf of the victims to increase their safety.

In a criminal matter, the goal of this EPO is to help prevent further abuse by the respondent (alleged abusing person) during the gap of time between the arrest and the court date. Each order is written specifying what type of personal contact is banned between the respondent and any family or household member. The order may also give "possession" of the residence to the petitioner (meaning that the respondent has to stay away from that same residence). If the terms of the order are violated, the offender can be arrested for violating this order of protection. This arrangement is temporary and does not affect any other legal rights.

I specifically remember one case where I was given the opportunity to appear before a magistrate to request an EPO.

It was the beginning of 2004, and downtown, the Saturday nightlife was in full swing, celebrating Mardi Gras.

Sometime around midnight I received a call to report to the Depot District, and when I did, I walked into an atmosphere thick with chaos, fear, and a lot of people.

A 32-year-old woman had left a bar to meet her estranged husband outside in order to exchange custody and pick up their 6-year-old daughter. When the woman approached his red convertible Corvette, the father and mother began arguing. Then things escalated and he grabbed her by the hair and pulled her halfway through the window. At that point, she started to scream, and two other men attempted to come to her rescue, one on each side of the car.

In the meantime, someone called 911. Just as the first officers arrived, the man who was standing next to the driver's side door took out a knife and began to slash through the canvas top of the convertible. To be expected, the police yelled for him to halt, when all of a sudden, the driver inside the car, who had entrapped his wife by her hair, now pulled out a gun and shot at the man with the knife, even while his young daughter was sitting on his lap. People began to panic and run everywhere.

The man was able to walk away from the car and was soon taken to University Medical Center, while the husband was arrested for aggravated assault and endangering the life of a child.

I don't frequent nightclubs and bars in the Depot District, a section of downtown well known for its nightlife, and I couldn't have chosen a more frenzied occasion for my first appearance. After I pulled up on Buddy Holly Avenue, it took me a few more moments to get through the crowd of tense people and find a couple of officers just outside The Daiquiri Lounge. In another minute or two, Corporal Neal Barron and Officer Chris Daniel informed me that while the husband had been taken into custody, the mother and child had been escorted by other officers to the back of the bar. Then they said, "Come with us."

With Officer Daniel in front of me and Corporal Barron behind, we three proceeded through this establishment literally packed with people. And although we were moving at a quick pace, I became uncomfortable and began to experience my own existential crisis. *How did I get here?* I thought. But then I also realized, *what do I have to be worried about? Here I am, guarded by these two, formidable, 250-pound, six-foot-three-or-something guys. And there are probably another dozen cops out on the street. This may actually be the safest place in Lubbock right now.* And so I was able to calm a bit and prepare for the business at hand.

Once we made our way to the back of the bar and into a separate room, I was introduced to the mother and her little girl. Both were extremely upset and frightened as they began to relay the distressing events of the night.

My foremost goal was to be that empathetic and calming presence in order to help alleviate their stress as well as calm them down. If I could succeed in doing that, I knew both mother and daughter would remember more clearly what had happened, and consequently, be able to provide a more accurate statement to the police.

Very soon, however, we decided the bar scene was just not the best place for mother and child. A better solution would be to move everyone to a more quiet and tranquil location. Ultimately, we left the decision up to the mother, and she chose to move our meeting to her office across town. There we were able to finish discussing the tragic encounter, and as we wrapped up our time together, I reminded her,

"Your husband is in jail right now, but there's a great chance he'll make bail and be out in the next 12 hours. That means we need to think about doing whatever we can to keep you and your daughter safe."

She asked about a restraining order, so I went on to inform her of temporary places where she could stay, what items she might want to retrieve from her house as well as when and how to do that, what to do about her daughter going to school the next week, and several other details with regard to their welfare and safety. I also introduced her to the notion of an EPO, informing her that this piece of paper signed by a judge would make it a crime for her estranged husband to be in her presence. I explained that in her case, it was more appropriate to request an EPO rather than a restraining order, which is used for civil matters, and which if ignored, would typically involve a punishment of only a fine.

The mother was totally in agreement, and together we worked out the details, stipulating that her husband could not come within 500 yards of her or her daughter's presence—be it at their home, at work, or at school. When we finished our discussion, the mother expressed her appreciation, and I could tell she was relieved that something proactive could be done.

My next step was to return to the police department to complete the request, and when finished, I went to find the officer who was writing the report on the shooting and Corvette stabbing incident in the Depot District that night.

"Officer . . ." I called out to him as I walked up to his desk, "I've got this EPO that should be filed as soon as possible. So, what do I do now?"

"Okay—good. You can come with me," he stood and waved his hand. "They're arraigning the husband at this moment, and we'll probably be able to talk to the judge as well."

Moments later, I was on my way over to the city jail, where the officer introduced me to the magistrate conducting the arraignment.

At one point the judge turned to me and asked, "Why should I grant this motion for an order of emergency protection?"

"Well sir, this 32-year-old mother and her 6-year-old daughter are in fear for their welfare and safety in light of her estranged husband's actions earlier tonight. This man pulled up outside The Daiquiri Lounge on Buddy Holly Avenue in the Depot District at about 11:00 p.m. His wife was still inside the bar when someone informed her that he was waiting outside in a parked car with his 6-year-old daughter. The mother was worried about going out to meet him alone, so she asked another male to accompany her, which he did. As I talked with her, she told me that when she went outside and leaned into the passenger side window to talk to her husband, he demanded that she get into the car. She refused to do so, and when she said, 'no,' he grabbed her by the hair and pulled her through the window into his Corvette. She started to scream for help, and at the same time, the car, which was in gear, started to roll. The guy who had joined her was able to reach in through the passenger-side window, place the gearshift into park, and then tried to get the husband to release her."

"At this time, another man came up to the driver's side door and kicked at that door a few times. This same guy then decided to draw a knife and proceeded to rip the canvas top of the car. By this time, the police were there and ordered the guy outside the car to drop the knife. Then seconds later, the father reached under his driver's seat and pulled out a pistol with his right hand. He then reached across his daughter who was sitting on his lap, and started to squeeze off rounds at the man with the knife through the driver's side window. At this point, the man with the knife backed off, and the husband got out of the car to pursue him. Meanwhile, their young daughter was in the middle of all this terror, while the mother was screaming, 'My baby's in here!' "

"The father of the child (and owner of the vehicle) was apprehended by the police and charged with aggravated assault and endangering a child. This woman now fears for her life and that of her child. Thus, the need for the EPO."

As soon as I finished talking, the judge said, "Thank you", and without further delay, and to my great relief, he signed that piece of paper. That was the first time I had filled out an EPO, much less been put before a judge as an advocate for the victim. I'm glad everything worked out the way it did, and I'm glad the woman also found a safe place to stay that night. Seems we all did the best we could with a difficult and dangerous situation.

CHAPTER TEN
STREET CRED

While working on my master's degree in Community Counseling, I took a career counseling course as well as a career test, which was to indicate the occupations that would best fit with my personality. My first result ... "plumber." Not interested. Also on the list of career recommendations ... "police officer." This was in the late 1990s, and at the time, I thought, *No way, I don't want people shooting at me.* I didn't realize it then, but these results actually revealed that I possessed the same values and personality characteristics of police officers who were happy with their job. Ten years later I began working with a police department. And yes, bring on the donuts, the gallows humor, extraordinary situations, and the adrenaline!

As a person, I am practical, sensible, reality-based, and an actions-have-consequences kind of guy—many of the same traits of a good police officer, and perhaps these characteristics are part of the reason I relate so well to the department and to its work.

I'm a different type of MHP. I don't have an agenda, a dogma that I must adhere to. I try to be forthright and honest. And I think these are qualities that officers often respect. If I don't know something, I admit it. I don't have anything to prove, so I don't have to use fancy book-learning language. If I'm helpful, that's great. If not, that's fine too. I know my job is an art and I have my limitations, too. I freely admit I'm not a police officer, and I don't try to do officer things (except arresting my 4-year-old when she's mouthy) and I try to do my part. I also acknowledge and appreciate how much these officers care about me, my safety, and our Crisis Team, as evidenced by the following story.

One Friday evening, as I was cruising around on a patrol shift, I was flagged down by a motorist whose windshield had been smashed by someone who had thrown a beer bottle while both cars had been driving down 34th Street. Subsequently, I called out on the radio to let Dispatch know where I was (34th and X) and that I was 10-46 (flagged down to assist a motorist). Once I learned what the motorist needed, I thought I'd be cool and use the radio code for "Send an officer over, no emergency." Well, that radio code happens to be "Signal 1." But instead, I called out "Signal 2," which basically means, "Help me! Help me! I'm being stabbed!"

As I let go of the button on my radio mic, I heard a few different officers respond on the radio…

"232 [an officer identifying himself]…where is he?"

"241…where is he?"

"211…where is he?"

"230 [a sergeant]…where is he?"

At that point, I thought, *Wow, that's a whole lot of fuss over simply asking for an officer to come take a report.* Then it hit me.

Straightaway, I grabbed the radio and quickly said, "Victor 1, no emergency; I just need an officer for a report."

Instantly, everything became quiet…until I returned to the department. The occasion of my mistake would not go unnoticed, and was too fine of a mess-up to ignore. As soon as I ran into some officers who had heard the entire conversation go down on the radio, they mimicked, "Signal 2—huh?" and couldn't resist giving me a hard time.

What I learned that night, however, was that I had a lot of people ready to rush to my rescue while I was on duty, and in time, I learned that the same applied for when I was off duty as well.

In my experience, most police officers are kind human beings who are called on to be tough at times. Yet, after dealing with a small percent of society who most people don't want to believe exist, and seeing those people commit crimes over and over again, officers and other EMS personnel tend to build up their psychological armor, or may even become calloused, because it is hard to survive emotionally in that environment. The cops in Lubbock are also taught at the academy how *not* to lose an argument, which goes over really well at home with a spouse. Likewise, they are taught to control a situation, which often comes off as arrogant or rude. I think if people understood the job—the pressures, the danger, the ugliness of what people can do to each other, how rude people can be to officers, and the recent frequency of ambush killings of law enforcement personnel—they might better understand why many officers come off the way they do on a traffic stop. Police officers are generally kind, compassionate, caring, and considerate individuals, but are often called upon to be decisive, protective, and sometimes forceful. And because of the things they have to do and see—they can become guarded, defensive, suspicious, and even depressed.

I've learned much about police officers, not only by working with them, but also by conducting a national survey about hostage negotiators, which actually revealed some interesting conclusions about all police officers, in general.

When I decided to do such a survey, I contacted a guy experienced in gathering statistics, and he said, "You're going to need 250 police officers to fill out the survey in order for it to be legitimate." Subsequently, in 2014, I contacted 440 of the largest federal, state, county, and city law enforcement agencies in the country. Of the 440 agencies and associations contacted, 173 agencies (39%) from 43 states responded. Six of the responding agencies (e.g., state patrols and county sheriff offices) indicated they did not have hostage negotiators. Of the 173 responding agencies, 147 (85%) agreed to participate in this research and provided a contact person. This contact person was then emailed the survey and told how to return completed surveys. Of the 147 agencies and negotiator associations that agreed to participate, 119 (81%) in 38 states returned 514 completed surveys. Most responses came from city police departments, but I was likewise grateful for a response from sheriff's offices and state patrols.

I asked the participants—active law enforcement personnel who also served as members of a hostage negotiating team—to complete a demographic questionnaire, answer questions about their experiences as a hostage negotiator, and describe their personalities as well as their emotional coping styles and decision-making practices.

Knowing as much as possible about the men and women who do this type of demanding, high-stress work would prove beneficial for the ongoing training and future selection of negotiators as well as for the health and longevity of all involved in a callout situation.

In the year 2014, I was given the opportunity to share the results and implications of this survey, as well as discuss the topic, "The Use of Mental Health Professionals in Law Enforcement and Hostage Negotiator Callouts" in such places as the California Association of Hostage Negotiators Annual Conference in Anaheim, the Texas Association of Hostage Negotiators Annual Conference in San Antonio, the Western States Association of Hostage Negotiators Annual Conference in Bellevue, Washington, (my hometown!) and the Regional Crisis Intervention Training Conference sponsored by the Washington State Criminal Justice Training Commission in Burien, Washington.

At these conferences, as well as at many other speaking engagements, I've often been asked, "How do counselors and cops get along in your department?" and I get to say that the Lubbock Police Department is a testament to the idea that mental health and law enforcement professionals can work together well. Not only has the assistance from the Victim Services Crisis Team been accepted and appreciated by many a patrol officer, but my work as a negotiating team member has been respected by the SWAT team as well.

Cases in which I've been able to make helpful suggestions and accurate predictions, such as the 2003 SWAT callout when Adam Cline killed his ex-girlfriend and then killed himself (see chapter 3) has helped to build my "street cred." And I greatly appreciate the consideration and acknowledgment of my involvement, especially when I noticed that the SWAT commander had added the following comment to his list of "Procedures to follow during a SWAT callout"—"Rely on Andy."

Street Cred

On one of these callouts, I was asked what to do about a young veteran who had barricaded himself inside a house, supposedly armed and suicidal, but who was being flippant, making sarcastic comments to our negotiators, and constantly hanging up the phone to take other calls. I said to the SWAT commander that we might try taking the "Bear" (the department's huge armored car), and park it in front of this guy's house, up on his lawn, and then have a negotiator start calling out commands over the P.A. The SWAT team did just that. And what do you know? All of a sudden, this guy decided to take us seriously, and a few officers jokingly dubbed me "the wizard" when, within the next few moments, the bad guy surrendered.

The truth is, I've learned so much more from the LPD than what I've been privileged to discuss here. I'm grateful for and truly enjoyed the training that I've been invited to attend alongside these officers.

During one session with the SWAT Team, I participated in what is called a "table top exercise." The team and I were sitting in a classroom, discussing whether or not to use lethal force in each of a number of scenarios.

For example, the following is one of the cases we reviewed that day:

> You [as an officer] respond to a SWAT callout and receive information that two suspects have taken numerous hostages inside a liquor store during a robbery. Patrol officers have the store surrounded. Five entry team members arrive ahead of you and stack an emergency rescue team at the rear of the business. No team leaders are on scene yet, nor is the SWAT commander. You set up on the white side with your rifle and observer. One suspect is looking out the doorway, attempting to locate officers. The suspect is holding a handgun to a hostage's head. You have a clear shot with a good backstop. Would you use deadly force? Yes or no? Explain your decision and justify your actions based on department policy, state law, and federal law.

Examples such as the one above generate a lot of interesting discussion because not everyone in the room immediately agrees with each other regarding what to do.

At some point during this tabletop exercise, it came my turn to answer first, and by this point I was almost an equal member of the team. The scenario was short and actually didn't require much thought. The story was clear-cut, involving only one gunman who had already harmed some people and clearly needed to be stopped because he was about to kill again. All necessary officers and commanders were present at the scene, and the subject could be taken out with a clear shot and at no risk to any other person. The instructor then asked me—the pacifist MHP professional from Bellevue, Washington, who had never held a gun—"So Andy, would you shoot, knowing all you know about policies and procedures and lethal force?"

"Yeah, shoot him." I said clearly. "And shoot him twice!" And the whole room of officers busted out laughing because it came from sweet little ole me. And through the laughter and in the spirit of the joke regarding the hug-it-out guy saying shoot the bad guy, one of the sniper guys asked the SWAT commander, "So if Andy says it's okay to shoot, we can shoot, right?"

In addition to training, I've also been given the opportunity to join the interview board when an officer is being considered for the team, and I'll sometimes accompany SWAT members when a warrant is being served.

On one occasion, after a warrant service, I was sitting in an armored car with several of the SWAT team, all of us still in our gear, and was listening to the guys just talking shop.

One of the sergeants, an officer well known for his forthright and direct manner, began describing an incident that had happened recently within the department. As usual, he was being very blunt and left no doubt as to his personal opinions. Any officer who had been around even for a short time knew that while he might have a legitimate beef, his cocksure attitude might rub people the wrong way. And once again, a group of us had a front row seat to his style of confrontation.

At one point, he described his conversation with another officer who had really irritated him because he wasn't seeing eye-to-eye with him. "This is just b--- s---," he complained. "And so I went to so-and-so and I told him what I thought. But he wasn't listening to me either. I don't know what his problem is. He just wasn't getting it. This is ridiculous...." And he continued along these lines for the next minute or two.

Meanwhile, all the other SWAT officers in The Bear were quiet, but listening. Finally, after he had finished laying out all his complaints, he paused and was noticeably waiting for someone to acknowledge or agree with him.

I thought, *Eh, why not,* and decided to speak up.

"So Sarge ... how was your delivery when you said all this to him?" (Everyone in that vehicle understood that what I was really saying was, "Maybe you did have a point, but perhaps your tone was your typical tone . . .")

There was another pregnant pause, and the officers started to smile a bit.

Then, not surprising to any of us, he spat out in his usual cordial manner—"F--- you, Andy." Instantly, everybody busted out laughing. And at that point I *knew* I had a place in The Bear.

CHAPTER ELEVEN
WHEN A COP HAS TO KILL

"The only thing necessary for the triumph of evil is for good men to do nothing."

—Edmund Burke

On Wednesday, May 7, 2014, after attending the morning half of training for the negotiating team at the police academy, a few officers and I decided to stop for lunch at Applebee's. We were enjoying messing with each other, talking shop, and were just about finished with our meal when we received a call from Sergeant Ross Hester, on duty as a patrol supervisor that day. "I think you guys better get ready," he said. "It looks like we may get called out."

Quickly, everyone paid their tab and then awaited the call. Hester called back. "Yeah, it's a go. Need you at 63rd and Avenue U."

While everyone else jumped into their patrol cars, I likewise drove off in my personal vehicle, made somewhat of an attempt to obey most traffic laws…and somehow arrived at the residence first. I grabbed my bag with all the necessary gear, threw on my tactical vest and helmet, and went to find somebody who knew what we should do next.

"What's shakin'?" I asked an officer I knew who was blocking one end of 63rd Street.

"Don't know. Lieutenant Mayne is over there. You can go ahead and ask him."

"Hey Lieutenant," I called out to Mayne as I made my way toward him, "is there anything I can do?"

"Yeah, Andy. Go on down the street to that house where Captain Hudgens is standing outside. Stand behind the guys with the guns and see what you can do."

"Okay, sure." I thought I'd better first inform the patrolman blocking the end of 63rd that I was going on down to the house, and after I returned to give him the information, I proceeded back down the street where I met with the captain and two civilians. I assumed they were the people who called this in, and this was their front yard.

I greeted the captain and said, "Well, what do you think I can do?"

"Sergeant Hester is already inside," he said. "Maybe you can go in there and help him out." Even while the captain was making this suggestion, Sergeant Hester came outside with an update.

The officers were able to convince the man inside, armed with two knives, to agree to hand over one of his knives in exchange for a bottle of water. Subsequently, a bottle of water was rolled to him, and a knife was tossed across the room in the back of the house.

I mentioned that I thought the trade was a good sign, and Sergeant Hester said, "Andy, why don't you come on in with me?"

Awesome. For approximately 13 years, I had trained as a negotiator and gained some significant experience on several callouts as a negotiating consultant. Usually, I was stationed at the command post, from where I continually passed along suggestions to the primary and secondary negotiators dealing directly with the subject(s). This time, when presented with the opportunity of conversing with a subject face-to-face, I was very comfortable and felt prepared. Hence, shortly before one o'clock in the afternoon, I stepped inside the residence with Sergeant Hester.

As I stood just inside the door of this trashed residence, somewhat to the side and behind Sergeant Hester, in what I think was an 8' x 10' living room, I could see through a doorway to a kitchen area, just a few steps away. Through the doorway and to the left, three officers were standing in a room off of the kitchen area. Two had pistols drawn while the third was holding a patrol rifle—and all three were pointing at a man I couldn't see, but who sounded extremely agitated as he talked with two of the officers.

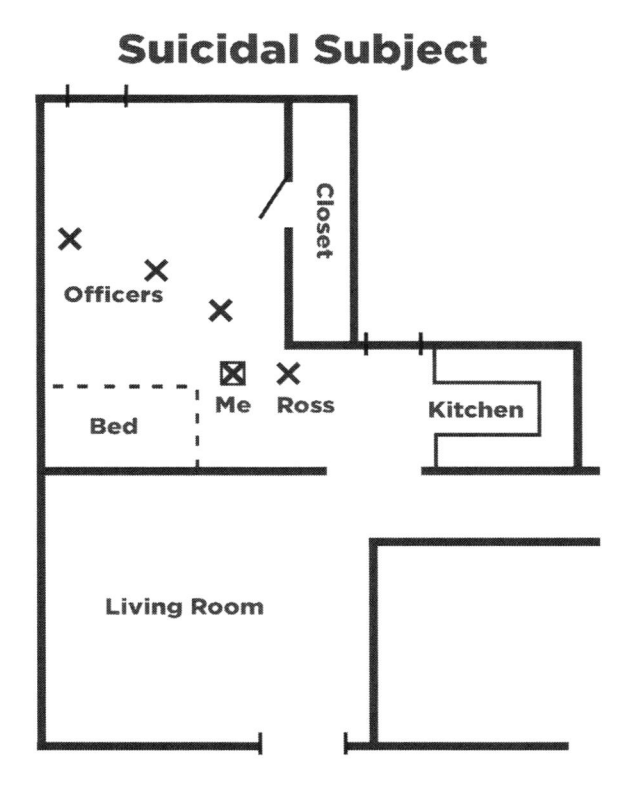

Suicidal Subject

Sergeant Hester and I entered the kitchen area and listened out of the view of the agitated man. As we listened to the conversation between the man and one officer, Sergeant Hester turned to me and asked, "What do you think?"

"I think the officer needs to lower his tone and calm down a little," I said quietly.

Immediately, Sergeant Hester turned and murmured that same advice to the officer speaking, and at once, the officer lowered his voice; likewise, the subject seemed to calm down a bit.

Following is a transcription of the negotiation/conversation with the subject. "M" represents the man with the knives, whom I will call "Mike" (not his real name, and because the name Mike is perfect for bad guys). "O" stands for any officer talking. "H" stands for Sergeant Hester and "A" represents me (Andy). Also included in parentheses are my own comments—sometimes a description of the situation, sometimes a description of Mike, and at other times I include my reasoning for the use of various responses.

* * *

O-1: Mike, put the knife down and let's talk about this. Come on, do the right thing, Mike. Put it down.

M: Is she here? (hallucinating)

O-1: No, she's not here. They're not going to let your mom in here because you're too agitated. We tried to tell you that.

M: I'm agitated because she f---ing ain't here.

O-1: That's right, you're not going to get to talk to her until you put the knife down and come on out. (Mike is standing in a closet.)

O-2: Don't come out of the closet, Mike. Put the knife down, Mike.

O-1: Your mom…your mom…you'll be able to talk to your mom in….

M: Why are you watching from the back? SWAT's already here. I'm outta here, man.

(Mike noticed that someone else had come inside the house. Sergeant Hester reentered the house, and I accompanied him.)

O-2: We've got negotiators here.

M: Okay, well, tell them to get out of here, man. They're f---ing… They're drilling through the f---ing walls.

O-1: They're not drilling through the walls.

M: And, there's f---ing wires along… You…go ahead and shoot me, man…

O-2: Don't come out of the closet, Mike. You're getting too close.

M: Hello? Hello?!

O-2: I don't want to have to hurt you. Don't come out of the closet any further, man. You got that knife. You're dangerous. Okay?

M: Aw, man. They're right behind that thing, man.

O-2: There's two other guys over here, okay. There's two other guys over here.

M: (incomprehensible arguing) …trying to get me…

O-2: The only other thing we want to do is get you to come out of there.

M: I ain't coming out of here until I talk to my mom, man.

O-3: (lowered, calmer tone) Do you want some more water?

M: Nope.

O-3: Are you sure?

M: No. … Does sound good.

O-2: Do you want some more? We can get you some more. Just water.

O-3: If you want some more, I'll get it, okay.

M: It's sharp.

O-3: No, I can get it. The neighbors are loaning it to us.

M: I said the knife's sharp.

O-3: Oh.

M: (tone raised and agitated again) No wires, man! What the f--- is that? You're trying to trick me, man!

O-2: (tone raised in response) Nobody is even back there.

M: Then why do you keep looking back over there? (The subject realizes that someone else, who he can't see, is in the house—Sergeant Hester and me.)

O-3: I'm looking at you.

M: No, him! You're trying to trick me, aren't you?

O-3: There's a negotiator standing right here.

M: No f…! I know, they're probably trying to trick me to get me to… no bullshit, tell him to come out.

O-3: Alright. This is Andy Young. He's a negotiator with the SWAT team. Okay?

(I step out so that the subject can see me, and I can see him standing in the closet. He has tattoos—in the shape of two diamonds on his face, with the bottom half of the diamonds below his eyes and the top half of the diamonds above his eyes—what I think looks like clown tattoos or something like the disturbed, chaotic look of the Joker in the Batman flicks. Throughout our conversation, Mike continues to open the closet door, peek out, rattle the knives, and then close the door again. His movements are furtive and his thoughts are everywhere.)

M: Why are they...?

A: I'm sorry? (Calm, relaxed, soft tone)

M: Why are they trying to get me right here with these f---ing things right here, man?

A: No, there's nothing there that's going to get you. ... He's with me. We're both doing the same thing for you.

M: It ain't a good day. (His tone calms)

A: No, it's not. Can you tell me about it?

M: Nah.

A: No?

M: I want to die.

A: Well, we don't want that. Okay? If you want to talk to your mom, all you got to do is put the knife down.

M: (mumbles) Nah.

A: Yeah, nobody wants to hurt you.

M: I can't talk to my mom...

A: You can talk to your mom, but you've got to put the knife down.

(Throughout the conversation, I try to grant his requests. First, I let him know that he will be able to speak to his mother.)

M: Get in those handcuffs, man, and then I'll talk to her from jail.

A: You want to talk to her later?

M: You're lying, man.

A: You're worried I'm lying to you?

M: I'm going to give up the knife, and I'm going to jail. No talking.

A: No talking to who?

M: To anyone. Right?

A: That's up to you.

M: No, I'm saying that's what's going to happen.

A: Well, you can talk to your mom before you leave this house.

(Second request: Mike can talk to his mom at his house rather than at jail.)

M: You're lying.

A: I've got no reason to lie to you.

M: You want to see a murder?

A: Not today. I've seen plenty. … Nobody wants to. Okay?

M: I do.

A: Why is that? Everything's going to look different tomorrow. (At this point, I have hope that we may be able to talk him into putting the knife down and coming with us. Sergeant Hester says something to me.)

M: Why's the black one trying to get right there, man?

A: He's with me.

O: This is Sergeant Hester. He's a SWAT negotiator.

(Sergeant Hester is wearing a vest that says, "Negotiator." He takes his helmet off in an attempt to calm the subject. I take off my helmet as well.)

H: Look. Look at me. Look, I'm a negotiator. I'm not SWAT. Okay? We're not a negotiator. I mean, I'm not SWAT. I'm a negotiator.

M: Gotta be the other…man. … I ain't going to prison.

A: We're standing here because nobody wants you to get hurt.

M: What's that?

A: He's talking about taking his helmet off.

H: See? See it's me, man. I'm not SWAT. SWAT wouldn't do that, right? … And that boy's back here with your water. Okay?

M: That's it, man. I ain't going back to no prison.

H: Why would you go to prison?

M: Why wouldn't I not? … Whacha tryin' to do? Tase me with that f…ing thing?

H: No, sir.

A: What do you see?

M: Something? He keeps looking down.

A: Alright, tell me what you see. What do you see? (I want to make sure he's grounded in reality.)

M: Well, I'm probably going to die. I'm probably going to die.

A: You know nobody wants that, right? Nobody wants to hurt you.

M: Probably not. Right? Try and hit me with that stun…

H: Mike, there's nobody else but us here.

M: It's over. It's gonna happen.

A: Don't let it happen. Don't let it happen. (I turn to Sergeant Hester.)

M: What'd you say?

A: We're just talking about how to help you.

M: How to help right here?

A: No, we're talking about how to help you. We don't want you to get hurt today.

M: (pained groan) Look…it hurt like a m--- er f---er.

A: What hurt?

M: I don't give a f--- about it hurting. I'll be in pain for the rest of my life. Jesus, forgive me…

A: Are you in pain right now?

M: (Obviously praying. He's now turned away from me and facing into the closet.) Forgive me for everything…

A: Mike, are you hurting?

M: (Continues to mumble and pray.)

A: Do you have children to take care of?

(I attempt to reach him by speaking of any children he might have, and I find out later that he does have children.)

M: (More mumbling and praying.)

A: Do you have children to take care of?

M: You're trying to get me to talk. It's over. (More pained groans.)

A: Are you hurting?

M: It's gonna happen. It's gonna happen.

A: Can you look at me?

(Asking him to look at me, I try to bring him into reality and keep him grounded, and hopefully derail him from his current track of wanting to die.)

M: I gotta build myself up, man. It's gonna happen.

A: Well, we don't want it to happen. Why do you want it to happen?

M: I don't want to sit in no f---ing holding cell today, man.

A: You don't want to be in a holding cell?

M: I don't want to go to no f---ing holding cell.

A: What do you want?

M: What I want, y'all can't give, man. I can't go back. You can't just let me free…

A: Well, we want you to go to the hospital.

M: You're going to take me to jail, man.

A: No, we want you to go to the hospital.

M: You just tried to give him the signal to shoot me with that thing, man.

A: Nobody wants to shoot you.

M: With that f---ing…whatever the f--- it is.

A: You talking about a taser?

M: Yeah.

A: We got an ambulance outside; we want to take you to the hospital.

M: I'm not getting shot by no f---ing taser, man.

A: That's fine. You've just got to put down the knife. We want to take you to an ambulance.

M: I'm going out in an ambulance. (sarcastic)

A: Yeah, we want to take you to an ambulance, but we don't want you hurt.

(The SWAT team enters the house.)

M: I'll be dead, I won't be hurt. … Something's going on man. There's too much air coming in that wasn't coming in before, man.

A: You feel air?

M: Yeah.

A: Where do you feel air coming from? This way?

M: Behind you, man.

A: From behind me?

M: You're trying to play with my f---ing head, man. (Mike becomes more agitated when he realizes that someone else [SWAT] has entered the house.)

A: Sir, I just want you to come out without the knife.

M: You're trying to f---ing play with my head, man.

A: No, sir.

M: Yeah, you are, man. (frustrated groan) What did you say?

A: They're just talking about what to do here.

M: Are they going to shoot me?

A: They don't want to shoot you. (The SWAT officers stand to my right, out of view.)

M: They're going to have to.

A: Nah, they don't want to.

M: Bring the f---ing … (mumbling), man.

A: They don't want to.

O: These officers don't want to do it.

A: SWAT doesn't want to do it either. Nobody wants you to get hurt.

M: Come on. Should have f---ing shot me. Go ahead and shoot me right here, man. There they are, they're SWAT, right? (The officer with the beanbag gun moves in front of me from my right to my left.)

A: Right, but they don't want to hurt you.

M: Is that a beanbag? Huh? Is that a beanbag or a shotgun?

A: We want you to come out with us. Just put the knife down.

M: Is that a beanbag or a shotgun? If that's a beanbag, I'm going to come out full throttle.

(As soon as I hear him say that he will be "coming out full throttle," I know that he is very serious about dying. There is what feels like a very long pause and everyone taking a breath. Even as I take my breath to start talking again, he yells and charges out into the room, running from my right to my left towards the patrol officer with the rifle. The officer with the beanbag gun shoots Mike in the left torso. Mike's momentum, however, carries him forward towards the officer across the room from the closet. Then two officers, one with a rifle and one with a pistol, shoot him at very close range. Mike falls down with obvious gunshot injuries. The SWAT officers quickly put down their rifles and move into position to administer first aid.)

End of transcript.

* * *

Days later, as I listened to the recording of this callout and thought back over what had happened, I had a few more realizations about the victim as well as myself. First, I was somewhat surprised by the look of the subject. But then again, I had never previously talked to a guy with clown tattoos on his face, high on meth, holed up in a closet, waving around a machete and another big knife, just a few steps away from a bunch of cops with their guns drawn.

As I thought about Mike charging out of the closet, that very instant reminded me of the pivotal scene in the movie *Tombstone* where the lawmen, played by Kurt Russell, Val Kilmer, and Sam Elliott, show up at the OK Corral. History records that at about 3:00 p.m. on Wednesday, October 26, 1881, in the town of Tombstone, the most famous gunfight in the Wild West went down between five western outlaws (known as the Cowboys) and four lawmen—Wyatt Earp, his brothers, and Doc Holliday.

In the movie scene, as men from both sides stare each other down in OK Corral, everyone is tensely still, knowing what is about to happen.

When a Cop Has to Kill

The character of Billy Clanton, one of the Cowboys (played by Thomas Hayden) sees the lawman, Doc Holliday (Val Kilmer) give somewhat of a cocky look and then a wink. At that point, Clanton's facial expression changes to deadly determination, and the character of Wyatt Earp (played by Kurt Russell), realizing what is about to happen, exclaims, "Oh, my God."

In the next second, the gunfight starts.

This moment of Earp's realization in the movie reminded me of the second there was complete silence in that small room, and we all sensed what Mike was about to do. That moment seemed to last a long time, but in reality was about two seconds. I simply had no time to say one more word.

In hindsight, if I had a little more time, I would have done what my friend Kevin Briggs advises. At one time, Sergeant Briggs, a retired California Highway Patrolman and negotiator, was responsible for talking people out of jumping off the Golden Gate Bridge. He tells of one call where he sensed that the man he was talking to was very near to taking a dive. He then did what he called, "clap to stop the countdown"— he clapped loudly and abruptly yelled, "Hey!" and shouted the person's name—to shock the victim back into coherence.

In my case, who knows? If I would have yelled, "Hey, Mike!" I might have temporarily stopped Mike from charging at the police; at the same time, I might have also scared the hell out of the SWAT team and other officers in the house, which is what Sergeant Briggs did to his superior, who was observing this callout, and to the man hanging off of the Golden Gate Bridge.

Right after the man I was talking to fell to the floor with gunshot wounds, I remember that the patrol officers exited the house, while four SWAT members remained inside and immediately put down their weapons and started administering first aid. They knew exactly what to do and I watched as they did all that could be done.

Meanwhile, I was still standing in the same spot. In fact, from the time I first walked into the house with Sergeant Hester until the incident was completely over, I had moved only two steps to the left when I revealed myself to Mike.

As the officers administered first aid and I gathered a couple of rifles to one location, a few other SWAT officers entered the house and went back to the kitchen, which was to my right.

One of them asked me, "Has this area by the kitchen been cleared? Has the house been cleared?"

"I don't know anything about the other side of the house," I replied. "And the backyard hasn't been cleared. We've been in this kitchen area for a while...and I think it's okay."

Within the next few minutes, these officers proceeded to investigate the rest of the house and verify that all areas were clear.

Eventually, fire and EMS reported to the scene and took the place of the SWAT officers trying to care for Mike's wounds and start an airway.

When I exited the house through the front door, I decided that my next responsibility as a Critical Incident Stress Management (CISM) counselor was to go speak with the three men who had fired their weapons. When I found Sergeant Hester, I asked, "So, where are the officers who had to shoot this guy?"

"They're each in a different patrol car right now," Sergeant Hester replied, "and we have them separated prior to giving their statements about this shooting."

Directly, I went to meet with each one for just a minute or two, checking to make sure they were okay. Afterwards, however, because I was at the scene of the shooting as well, no one was quite sure what to do with me. Many times, as part of the Victim Services Crisis Team (VSCT), I will write a report about the work I've done with a victim. In this case, it seemed a VSCT report was not quite what was warranted.

At this point, my plate was full and then some. Mike's family was on scene, and would soon be transported to the police department to give statements about what happened that day. Another reason I couldn't meet with them was because of what I'd just witnessed and been a part of. So I was blessed to be able to call in members of the

VSCT to meet with the family and be with them. Tim, Janiece, and others accompanied the family and were with them when they found out that Mike had died. That part alone—was a tough part of the day.

Eventually, it was decided I should be accompanied to the police station, where I likewise typed a statement regarding the incident, and submitted it to a homicide detective.

After I finished, I ran into the chief of police, who asked me to come to his office. He was so kind when he asked how I was doing after such a thing. I told him I'd seen plenty of death and trauma, but had never witnessed the shooting death of a person, so I was still processing. One of the things still with me was the ringing in my ears from the loud gunfire, and the buzzing in my brain from a little sensory overload. This all began to subside as I wrote my statement, and subsided a little more as the chief and I chatted.

Another aspect of this callout that deserved reflection had to do with the fact that I am not a police officer. I am a civilian, and although I have attended negotiator training with police officers, I've been to a number of SWAT team trainings as an observer. I am, nevertheless, a civilian and probably should not have been in that house. Later, as the SWAT commander and I talked about this call, he shared that all the officers in that room were too close to the subject and, had we had more time, we would've needed to move out of the room while continuing to talk to Mike.

A few weeks after this incident, as I was having breakfast with the chief of police (previously a negotiator commander), our conversation turned toward this particular case. I wanted to know what he thought about my being in that room.

"So, Chief, do you think it was a mistake that I was in that house?" I asked.

He was kind and let me know that was not why we were having breakfast. And I knew that, but I also wanted to know his view on my being in that room.

He answered, "Yes, Andy, I do—for a couple of reasons. First, if anything had happened to you, it would have devastated everybody in the police department. A civilian should never be in the vicinity with anyone who has knives, guns, or any other weapon. Second, everyone in the room of that house was too close to the guy with the knife—even the officers were too close. The guy who charged was only a few steps away from them. And finally, though we discovered that there were no other weapons in the house, at that time we had no idea what exactly was in that closet."

I nodded, knowingly. But the chief knows me well . . .

"And yes, Andy…I know what you're going to say—you wanted to be there."

And he was right. Yes, I wanted to be there. I was suited up, and I felt safe with the officers in front of me and beside me. Still, I had to acknowledge that it was dangerous because we, indeed, did not know what else was in the closet with Mike.

Because I wanted to be clear, I followed up by asking him about the next time I would have to face a situation like that. Eventually, the chief said, "Andy, all things being equal, don't do that again. You simply can't get that close to something like that. And if you have any questions about what to do on the next one, feel free to call me."

"Yes, sir."

As I listened to the tape of the conversation, I was once again convinced of the mercy that was shown. When Mike's family learned that he had been shot, and shot more than once, they were quite upset. Yet when they listened to the tape of the conversations between Mike and our officers and negotiators, they realized that he had been given many opportunities to receive help and that we tried our best to talk him out of charging at the police. Consequently, the family's attitude changed 180 degrees. They also recognized that because Mike had deliberately threatened and charged the police, the officers had no choice but to shoot him—an action commonly termed as a "suicide by cop."

There are people who ask, "Why can't a police officer shoot a weapon out of the criminal's hand instead of shooting the criminal himself?" Or they ask, "Is it really necessary to shoot a person so many times, even though dangerous or armed, in order to stop them from hurting someone else?"

Many people believe that a bullet can stop a person as soon as he or she is hit just one time. But the one-shot drop scenario is an illusion. The fact is that one gunshot rarely stops a person. When discussing this subject, I often refer to an article entitled, "One-Shot Drops: Surviving the Myth," published in the October 2004 issue of the *FBI Law Enforcement Bulletin*.

For ten years, authors Pinizzotto, Kern, and Davis studied the use of deadly force against an officer as well as an officer's struggle to use deadly force in return. They interviewed many officers who attended the FBI National Academy during one of the four 10-week sessions held each year on various criminal justice subjects.

This article describes a case where a police officer was being charged by a disorderly subject, who was firing two guns at the officer. In reaction, the officer shot twice, hitting the man in the center of his chest. Yet the subject kept shooting and killed the officer by shooting him in the head. Although the officer hit the charging subject first, it was the officer who died. Why did this happen?

To answer the question—"Why does any officer die in the line of duty?" the authors considered the type of weapons issued to officers, the type of ammunition, the quality of self-defensive training officers receive, possible overconfidence in wearing a bullet-proof vest, the officers' physical condition, and other factors. They discovered at least two primary reasons that officers are killed on the job. First, there is a "significant hesitancy on the part of many officers to use deadly force."[20] Second, officers "stop shooting before they neutralize the threat."[21]

Yet much of the public thinks that if a gunman shooting at a police officer is hit anywhere in the torso, he or she will be immediately

---

20 Anthony J. Pinizzotto, Ph.D., Harry A. Kern, M.Ed., and Edward F. Davis, M.C. "One-Shot Drops: Surviving the Myth," *FBI Law Enforcement Bulletin*, Federal Bureau of Investigation, U.S. Department of Justice, October 2004, p. 15.

21 Ibid.

stopped. This is not true and often ends in the good guy's own death. In the same article quoted above, the authors describe a specific case where a subject fired at an officer, and the bad guy was subsequently hit 13 times by two officers in return. Still, the offender was able to run for another several blocks.

I've personally responded to a call where a guy shot himself with a .38 in the center of his forehead. The bullet then went under his skin, hit his skull, traveled around between the skin and the skull, and finally exited out the back of his head. What were the extent of his injuries? He suffered only flesh wounds.

Likewise, much of society has no understanding of what an officer faces when making the critical decision to shoot someone, and many people will make judgments about an officer shooting without having all the facts. Even eyewitness testimony can often be unreliable; and sometimes, unfathomably, people will lie to promote their agenda, or use the incident for their own purposes or to make a point. I have discovered that you can never—never—judge a situation by watching a news clip or by listening to or reading any type of news media (much less trusting firsthand eyewitnesses as they describe what happened in front of a news camera). The media rarely, if ever, has all the facts; yet television, radio, and newspaper reporters imply that they speak authoritatively about what has happened—even at the expense of innocent lives.

While the officials within our law enforcement and judicial systems attempt to sort through a chaotic or criminal situation, they cannot immediately reveal all the details. These officials, more often than not, are not trying to hide the facts; rather, they are doing their job. Usually, chiefs of police, public relations officers, information officers from law enforcement agencies, or district attorneys will say something along the lines of, "Presently, we are investigating. Please give us time to collect all the facts and allow us to do our job." These facts cannot be gathered in seconds or minutes, even in this day of social media where, literally, the entire world can be informed of an event while it is occurring.

Many people lack understanding about such a crisis, whether it's an officer-involved shooting or any other traumatic event. Specifically, people are unaware or choose to ignore that inherent truth about a crisis: crisis is *instant chaos* and *emotionality*, whereas the facts emerge *slowly* and *over time* and are a *cognitive* entity.

There are two important elements of emotion. Number one: Emotions are not facts. Number two: Emotions inhibit perception and memory. Therefore, it is only after all the chaos and the emotions settle down that the truth can be revealed. People are then faced with a choice—to accept that truth or to continue believing what they want to believe—even if it's dead wrong. Unfortunately, much of the public is not interested in the truth or in the facts so that justice can be served. Many are more interested in judgment—and swift judgment—whether it's deserved or not. And some are only interested in their agenda and are looking for places that set a stage for their agenda to be heard.

At the same time, some people continue to ask silly or even ridiculous questions, such as, "Why didn't the officer jump out of the way, or shoot out the front window, the tire, or the radiator, instead of killing the driver?" A driver who was charging full speed toward the officer with a 3,000-pound weapon, fully intent on killing him, should not expect to have his radiator shot. Undoubtedly, if this officer who was faced with imminent death hesitated, it would have been his own life that he would have sacrificed. But even when the officer survives, he may not feel as though he made the right decision. This is especially true when he suffers from the trauma of killing someone and from dealing with so many people in the court of public opinion who are now seemingly against him. Despite being well trained in the use of a firearm, officers are not often trained in how to deal with the pain, grief, cognitive dissonance, and mental struggle associated with being forced to kill another person.

Nevertheless, there are also many of us who realize the debt we owe to brave police officers, and encourage them to stay the course. As the authors, Pinizzotto, Kern, and Davis, so aptly wrote:

Employing deadly force against another human being is not an easy choice, nor should it be. However, when an individual is intent on causing grave bodily injury, even death, to officers sworn to uphold this nation's laws, those officers must react responsibly and quickly to protect their communities and to avoid the loss of innocent lives, as well as their own. The perpetuation of the one-shot drop by movies and television programs has no place in the real world of violent criminals bent on their destructive missions. Officers must realize that they have to continually hone their survival skills, always expect the unexpected, and never give up; they must protect themselves to protect their communities.[22]

---

22   Ibid, p. 21.

CHAPTER TWELVE
HELPING THE GOOD GUYS COPE

In the West Texas town of Odessa, about two hours south of Lubbock, Corporals Arlie Jones, 48; Abel Marquez, 32; and John Scott Gardner, 30, were shot in the line of duty during the early evening hours of Saturday, September 8, 2007. All three officers would die as a result of the attack. A day later, after news of the horrific outcome reached our police department in Lubbock, we were asked to provide Critical Incident Stress Management (CISM) assistance and made plans to immediately travel to Odessa. In the meantime, I was informed of the details of this disastrous situation.

When Officers Arlie Jones and Abel Marquez first responded to a disturbance call at about 6:30 p.m. the night before, a woman met them outside her house and informed them that she had been struck by her husband who had been drinking and was still inside. The two officers also were aware that her husband had access to various weapons, including a knife and several firearms.

At first, they decided to knock at the front door, but upon receiving no response, they proceeded around the house to the backyard. And that's when the bad guy opened fire with a 12-gauge shotgun. Marquez was hit in the neck, Jones shot in the head.

Somehow, Marquez was still able to talk and send out a call for help on his radio. In response, another group of officers quickly arrived, including Sergeant Pete Marquez, who found his brother, Abel, slumped near a patrol car, and helped him into another car that would rush him away. AeroCare then flew Abel to a hospital where he was later pronounced dead.

Meanwhile, another group of officers, including John Scott Gardner, were sent to the back of the house. But all too soon, even as Gardner was edging along the back wall, he was also shot in the head. At this point, two officers, Jones and Gardner, lay in the backyard, and now the other responding officers were faced with a terrible dilemma: should they risk their lives to attempt an officer rescue, or should they stay behind cover and not get killed themselves?

Gunfire continued, and SWAT teams responded from the Midland Police Department, Ector County Independent School District, as well as the Odessa Police Department. Four hours later, the shooter inside the house, who had been slightly wounded, finally decided to surrender and walk out the front door…but only after three officers had been horrifically slaughtered.

For the 73 years of its existence, the Odessa Police Department never had an officer fatally shot in the line of duty. But now, not only the department, but the entire city, was grieving.

In response, I, along with a group of police officers from our department in Lubbock, drove two hours south on Sunday, September 9th, in order to conduct a number of psychological debriefings and assist with the great mental and emotional toll.

That same day, we met with all types of emergency services personnel, most of which were police officers. Earlier, I had assumed the toughest intervention we would encounter would be the debriefing held with the three responding SWAT teams…but I had underestimated just how challenging it would be.

In a room at the police department sat approximately 40 SWAT officers. These officers were not just angry about what had happened to their fellow officers, they were flat-out infuriated—pissed off at the shooter, mad at themselves, outraged with their superiors, and mad at the situation. They had absolutely no interest whatsoever in working through how they felt about the situation and its outcome. Many were mad at everything and anything that moved…and they were determined to stay that way.

Their reaction wasn't surprising, nor did I think it inappropriate or wrong. It was just a fact. As I wrote in chapter 7, as well as in other parts of this book, there's really no such thing as a "right" or a "wrong" way, a "normal" or "common" way to react to a crisis. Any reaction can be expected. And certainly, in this case, anger—extreme anger about what had happened to three of their fellow officers—took no one off guard.

Everyone at that meeting was fully aware that brutality against police officers had been increasing throughout the country, and I was not surprised to read that the horrific news of this case made headlines a month later in *USA TODAY.*

On the front page of this paper, Kevin Johnson wrote, "Their [the three Odessa officers'] deaths are part of a rising number of fatal police shootings across the nation that have led police officials and law enforcement analysts to suggest that an increasing number of suspects are adopting a troubling disregard for cops. Miami Police Chief John Timoney describes the phenomenon as an emerging 'hunter' mentality among criminals. … Police officials from departments across the country say they are confronting more combative suspects in situations ranging from robberies to routine traffic stops. 'There is a basic lack of respect for authority,' says [Texas Ranger Capt. Barry] Caver. … 'It seems like there is a brutality and a willingness to cross a line, to take a life, even if it is a police officer.' "[23] And this was written in 2007!

Johnson also noted "at least one-third of the 60 [for 2007] were shot in the neck or head…. The location of the wounds, some police

---

23   Kevin Johnson, "As Slayings of Cops Rise, a New Brutality Surfaces," *USA Today* (October 15, 2007), pp. 1-2a.

officials say, could suggest the suspects had lethal intent because many officers wear body armor that better protects their torsos."[24]

The 40-some officers sitting in that room in Odessa were fully aware that this attitude among criminals was a growing problem, and it was no wonder they were enraged. Even so, I had a job to do. At the same time, having previously presided over dozens of debriefings with law enforcement and emergency services personnel, I could tell that this one was not going well. And all too soon, the atmosphere went from bad to worse. Many of these very angry SWAT guys started to turn on each other with criticism and accusation. And at that point, I decided we had to shut the meeting down.

Meanwhile, in the midst of the heated arguments and chaos, three police officers from Lubbock with whom I had traveled, were quietly standing by, watching me trying to lead this train wreck. Two of those officers, Jimmy Pachall and Johnny Hutson (also trained in CISM), responded to the SWAT callout in 2001 and were two of the team who had been positioned next to Sergeant Kevin Cox when he was accidentally shot and killed. These two men had experienced what every officer sitting in that room was now feeling and had likewise attended a similar debriefing.

When the anger in the room seemed to take a breath, I asked for everyone's attention. Then I said something along the lines of, "It's obvious we can't go any further with what I intended today. But before we adjourn, I'd like these two officers to say a few words." I briefly introduced Jimmy and Johnny and then sat down.

Instantly, the entire room went from a blatant outrage to a respectful silence. Everyone there knew of these two men and all were aware of what they had experienced in 2001. Now Jimmy and Johnny had their undivided attention.

Both officers stepped up and shared openly and in detail about the ordeal of losing a fellow officer and friend. In addition, they explained how they coped, and what they had to do to manage the pain. They confessed that at first, they weren't able to or perhaps had refused to

---

24   Ibid, p. 2a.

talk to people about how the situation was affecting them. And it may have taken them a while to ask for and receive help. Nevertheless, they admitted that once they acknowledged their need and accepted assistance provided by family, friends, and others, they began to heal.

Watching that room full of infuriated SWAT members, mad enough to burn anything and everything down, go from a furious 100 miles per hour…to zero…was an amazing thing to behold. From where I stood, these 40 officers didn't just casually or partially accept the suggestions from the officers of Lubbock, but *fully* received what they had to say.

When both men finished speaking, I thanked them and then wrapped up the meeting, letting the officers know we would hang around to speak one-on-one.

"We'll be hangin' around for a while," I offered, "and available if anyone would like to talk. Otherwise, please feel free to go."

In response, most of the officers stayed in that room and talked for quite a while with Jimmy and Johnny. Once again, I got to supervise from the side of the room and hold up a wall.

In most cases CISM helps—significantly—not only for emergency services personnel trying to cope with tragic circumstances, but for anyone seeking relief and healing after experiencing a traumatic, painful, or devastating incident. And one reason it does was clearly on display that day in Odessa—CISM is peer-driven, which means the heart of a CISM team is trained officers who do the same work as those who are currently in need.

* * *

As the Clinical Director for the CISM team of our police department, I'd like to share a few important notes about this type of stress—critical incident stress—and the training we offer to officers and mental health professionals so that they can help other emergency services personnel.

Critical incident stress is a type of stress that is caused by *any event* that has significant emotional power, or is so unusual that it overloads a person's or group's *ability to cope.*

Some examples of "critical incidents" that are discussed in our training include:

- Line-of-duty death.
- Injury to or death of a large group of people.
- Injury to or death of children.
- Experiencing a situation that is visually and/or audibly grotesque, or one with a horrible/disgusting smell.
- Co-worker suicide.
- Excessive media coverage; ops gone bad—big mistakes; long-term or physically demanding ops.

When we talk about stress in our lives, we think of our life as a balance beam. At one end, there's no stress. We call this end the "brown-out." At the other end of the beam, there is a lot of stress, and at this end we experience "burnout." In the middle of the balance beam is "general stress"—the everyday challenges and successes that actually make life worthwhile.

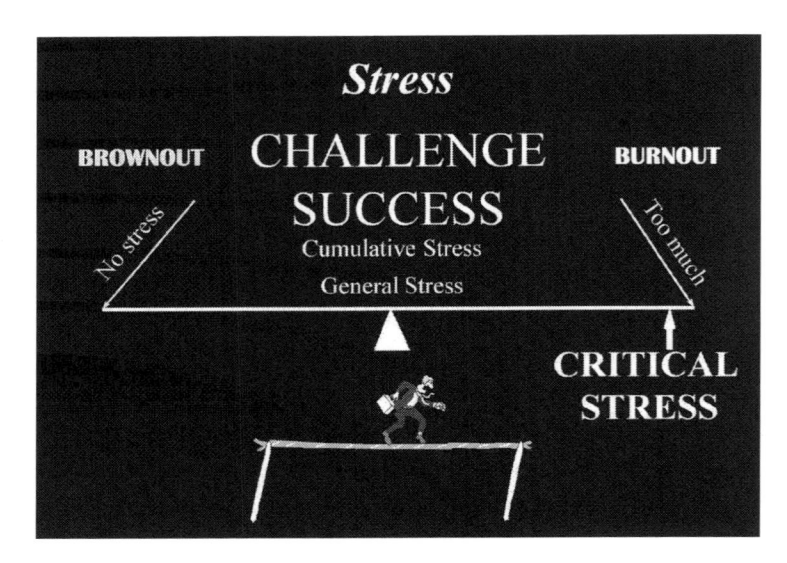

Ordinarily, with regard to general stress, people do pretty well by employing their own individual coping skills and are thus able to maintain balance in their lives. Even when the general stress increases, most people are able to adjust and maintain calm.

But suddenly, without any warning, a *critical* incident occurs, and the stress from that situation weighs heavy on the end of the beam (life), so that now, it is no longer in balance. That's when we recommend a CISM intervention—help given by *peers* so that the affected officer or person can return to their job and their life's routine as soon as possible, maintaining their usual performance level even in the face of a difficult event. This is crucial for the officer, their family, friends, other people they know, and for the department.

Although debriefings are conducted *after* our officers or staff members experience a traumatic incident, CISM is not therapy or a type of treatment for Post-Traumatic Stress Disorder. Rather, it is about *prevention*. The goal is to manage the stress so that the officer can return to duty without suffering the adverse effects of critical incident stress. Every meeting is confidential and private. What's said in the room stays in the room, and any reaction or response to the incident is considered normal.

During our own CISM training, and as we discuss how people react in different ways to stress, we refer to the statement made by Viktor Frankl in his book, *Man's Search for Meaning*, and I quote it here again: "An abnormal reaction to an abnormal situation is a normal reaction."[25]

Many symptoms of critical incident stress include:

- Tension (anxiety)
- Fatigue
- Sleep disturbances
- Change in diet

---

25 Viktor E. Frankl, *Man's Search for Meaning* (Boston, MA: Beacon Press, 1959), 20.

- Nausea
- Recurring memories/flashbacks
- Negative feelings like irritability, depression, or anxiety
- Self-blame
- Interpersonal problems

Again, the people and their symptoms are normal, while the situation is abnormal.

Some officers, like individuals of any occupation, don't want to think about or feel anything as a result of the pain. They'd rather just put it away. First, they find ways to shut off their thoughts; then, they close off their emotions. In many cases, you could say they get stuck somewhere in between, which can affect their thought processes and reactions. Thus, it is very important to help them begin talking in the days immediately following the incident.

In our CISM training for police officers as well as MHPs, we specifically address how an officer may attempt to cope. Research shows that 75 percent of officers are able to return to normal functioning using their own coping mechanisms. While these ways of coping may be different for each officer, he or she will often choose whatever enables them to deal best with the stress—humor, exercise, sleep, etc.

Another 25 percent of officers will attempt to use coping mechanisms that are not sufficient (alcohol, denial, regression, etc.). Some officers may not attempt to cope at all, but rather avoid. Consequently, they are not able to return to normal functioning. In the short term, this may simply mean their thinking processes and emotions are affected. In the long term, an officer may develop Post-Traumatic Stress Disorder.

The CISM team within our police department is made up of individuals of three different professions: mental health professionals who handle the mental aspects of assistance and also help with referrals when required; police officers or peer-support personnel, chosen because of their operational background; and possibly a chaplain.

Officers who attend CISM education understand before experiencing any traumatic incidents the kind of negative and/or cumulative stress they might incur on the job as well as what kind of assistance to expect from a department concerned with their well-being.[26]

In addition to the pre-incident training, our CISM assistance is provided via five avenues:

1. On-scene assistance. CISM is provided immediately after the crisis occurs—even at the scene, especially if extremely traumatic. These cases include the shooting of, an injury to, or the death of an officer; or, when an officer has injured or killed someone else in the line of duty. Chaplains can be particularly good in this role.

2. Demobilization. A demobilization is a short meeting—perhaps ten minutes—conducted immediately after major incidents, when officers or EMS/fire crews may benefit from learning about coping skills to get them through until a defusing or debriefing can be conducted. The purpose of this meeting is also to help participants make the transition from working the crisis to going home.

3. Defusing. A defusing is a meeting approximately 30 minutes to one hour in length. This is the most commonly used CISM process and is less formal than a debriefing. The defusing usually occurs very shortly after people get off their shift following an incident. A timely defusing can often preclude the need for

---

26 For more about CISM within police departments and other law enforcement agencies, please see the article, "The Effectiveness of Cumulative Stress Debriefings With Law Enforcement Personnel," published in the *International Journal of Emergency Mental Health* (January 14, 2014), in which I further assess the benefits of therapeutic group meetings with on-duty police officers attempting to process and cope with the stress associated with police work.

a longer debriefing because it provides participants with a forum for quickly processing a traumatic event.

4. Debriefing. A debriefing is a meeting held within 24 to 72 hours after the incident (except for line-of-duty deaths) and can last anywhere from one to four hours. It is a group intervention for those directly affected by the incident and provides a forum for more in-depth psychological processing of the facts, perceptions, thoughts, and reactions to the event. It also provides more information about coping.

5. Follow-up. Our CISM team members also provide follow-up and referral after the formal CISM process is over.

In every instance of CISM intervention listed above, one-on-one interaction is an important key to our LPD CISM team. We respond to help individual officers as needed, on scene as well as after they leave the scene. We're also available to those people who don't want to talk in a group setting, or for those who come to a team member privately after the group process has concluded.

The CISM process is no different for any of our other first responders who also need to reduce the amount of emotional baggage they accumulate through careers that can be loaded down with stressful incidents. The worst thing people can do is to let those experiences ruminate or fester.

Even with all the previously mentioned interventions in place, some officers may continue to experience adverse side effects. Our police supervisors are instructed to be aware of an officer's increased use of sick leave, a surge in citizen complaints about the officer's performance, or a decrease in work productivity. Likewise, if an officer seems to be withdrawing from peer interaction or other social functions, appears down, increases his alcohol consumption, or is having marital problems—help can be offered.

Unfortunately, it's a fact that, too often, police officers must respond to scenes of tragedy and emergency calls of a horrific nature—abuse of children, domestic violence, stabbings, gross physical or mental trauma, trapped victims, kidnappings, homicides, aggravated sexual assaults, death, and serious injury. Part of their job is facing dangerous and life-threatening situations as well as working hard to keep people safe.

Yet, I think, even today, much of the general public is somewhat indifferent to the life of a police officer (many of whom have families and children of their own) and underestimates the potential hazards they face on a daily basis.[27]

So, I often take the opportunity to emphasize the grave importance of offering help and intervention, such as CISM, to our officers and other EMS personnel. It behooves us to take very good care of the men and women who constantly take good care of us.

---

[27] For more information I recommend the books, *Emotional Survival for Law Enforcement: A Guide for Officers and Their Families* by Kevin Gilmartin and *I Love a Cop* by Ellen Kirschman.

CHAPTER THIRTEEN

WHY AM I STILL DOING THIS?

> *"It is true that decent people form a minority. More than that, they always will remain a minority. And yet I see therein the very challenge to join the minority. For the world is in a bad state, but everything will become still worse unless each of us does his best."*[28]
> —Viktor Frankl, Austrian psychologist
> Holocaust survivor

Today, I am part of a team boasting nearly 40 members—decent people who are proud to work with the Lubbock Police Department and give their best as they respond to those suffering tragic circumstances. We come with a vast background of experience and education in mental health and are employed in various positions of social work; counseling; child protective services and other state programs; and include graduate and doctoral interns as well. Being able to assist somebody on what is possibly the worst day of his or her life is something we all take very seriously.

---

28 Viktor E. Frankl, *Man's Search for Meaning* (Boston, MA: Beacon Press, 1959), p. 154.

In 2007, our Crisis Team changed from volunteer status to paid workers via a contract approved by our city council, and which is reviewed for potential renewal every three years. The police department (approximately 425 officers in 2015) has been very supportive and appreciative, to say the least. During the past 15 years, our caseload has increased to the point where we now respond to approximately 150 calls annually, but what has not changed is the weekend routine. Every Friday and Saturday night from 7:00 p.m. to 2:00 a.m., a team of two MHPs get in one of our city cars and patrol Lubbock, responding to calls at the request of the police, just as I did when I started in the year 2000. Of course, our team is also available 24 hours a day, every day of the week. I'm a lowly administrator much of the time, so I often relay calls from Dispatch via my cell phone, but I will occasionally take a call myself, and always hog the negotiator and SWAT callouts.

These days, as the program coordinator, I am busier than ever interviewing possible candidates for the team. When hired, each person trains with an assigned veteran crisis intervention counselor. Our prospective team members usually spend three to six months in field training before becoming a permanent member. I also continue to conduct CISM debriefings, not only for police and SWAT officers, but also for firefighters; paramedics; hospital and emergency medical staff; and for any employees who have experienced some sort of trauma, such as bank tellers or flight crews. In the meantime, I enjoy teaching an array of psychology, counseling and criminal justice courses at Lubbock Christian University (LCU).

I'm often asked if I ever struggle with burnout or if I find myself becoming somewhat hardened in order to deal with so much tragedy. Certainly, there are times when I, like many people, try to do too much, help too much, or overextend myself. But I've learned to set boundaries. I'm determined that my responsibility as a husband and father must come first and be set above everything else. If I don't have anything left when I get home, then I know I've done something wrong during the day.

Yes, I often see and deal with all manner of darkness, depression, gore and death; but in these horrible situations, I also witness redemption, healing, and love. Meanwhile, my full-time professor gig is a nice counterbalance, a career rated with high job satisfaction and low stress. For me, preparing lectures, doing some research, grading papers, and dealing with student complaints is at the other end of the tension-and-strain spectrum when compared to putting my fingers in head wounds and watching officers pull people off bridges.

With that thought in mind, I find it most fitting to conclude this book with an experience that combines both my passions—lecturing as a professor about my experiences as a crisis intervention counselor, negotiator, and CISM team member.

Following is a transcript of the address I presented in 2014 to a group of several hundred students at LCU when asked to speak in chapel on the topic: "Finding Your Vocational Passion."

* * *

At first, I was tempted to stand up here, put on a headset and microphone, and do my best impression of a motivational speaker. But as soon as I began to research the topic of vocational passion, I was assaulted by all that is out there on this topic, such as finding your personality, discovering your values, boundaries you should establish, dealing with burnout, creating diverse interests, learning to be happy in your job, and even more. Needless to say, the task became overwhelming.

Many of these categories reminded me of episodes of the television sitcom, *The Office,* or other comedic depictions of people attempting to find happiness in their jobs or with themselves.

I became somewhat discouraged when trying to think of what I had to say that would be worthwhile about an overdone, popular-culture-saturated topic. So I gave up that idea and instead decided to review my own vocational journey, which meant conducting some research about my own occupation as a college professor.

Consequently, I discovered that college professors, compared to a lot of other jobs, are people who are highly satisfied with their jobs, and at the same time deal with very low stress. Which led me to another despairing thought—how in the world, as a professor, can I talk to a group of people about creating a passion for their own vocation when I've never had to work at drumming up zest for a job that's comparatively great to that of everyone else?

So I had to move on to a third idea—my other job. My job as a counselor, a counselor at the scene of a crisis, working with the Lubbock Police Department; it has been a difficult, demanding, and draining job at times. Yet, I've been doing this job for almost 15 years and have no plans to resign. I have repeatedly seen horrible things for a long time, but still, I love this job.

Today, my hope is that through the telling of my vocational journey, and how I've had to find my way to maintain a passion in the most horrific of jobs, you will find something you can take back to your life.

I want to start by noting that I think *vocation* should also be defined as a "calling." It shouldn't be just about having a job or a career. More importantly, it's having a *calling*.

I'm a God guy. I blame Him for how I got here.

I blame Him, because after several years, I still have a passion for my calling.

It seems a part of my calling, for a long time, has been helping people. That might sound noble and all, but at times, it has been incredibly depressing, difficult, boring, and even ordinary. I knew early on that my calling was to help people, so I used my rational mind and got a Bible degree from LCU. I applied for and worked at internships where I could help people during the summers, and I was very passionate about that work. Once I finished, I didn't feel as prepared as I wanted to be; so I went on to ACU (Abilene Christian University) and got some more school. I want to note that those two years in Abilene, Texas were the loneliest, desert-type years I've ever experienced. But I made it through and finished.

Once I completed my master's degree in Youth and Family Ministry, and Abilene was happily in my rearview mirror, I interviewed many places. And...I struck out.

Eventually, I accepted a job at the Emergency Shelter of the Children's Home of Lubbock. Do you know what it's like to take care of abused children after they have been taken away from their mom? It almost made me long for the desert of Abilene—kind of like the Israelites longing for the great slavery gig in Egypt when they were wandering in the desert.

I remember driving around the Loop at 5:30 in the morning every day and praying the same prayer—"Oh, God, get me out of here."

And after about a year, He said, "Okay"—but not until I'd witnessed plenty of emotional carnage perpetrated on many children and received my own share of cuts and black eyes. I say all this to illustrate my first point about finding your vocational passion. And that is...

Suffering.

We all know that suffering is part of the deal. Even so, accepting it and understanding it is hard. People have to figure it out for themselves. You can't cheat off my test. In other words, I've had to learn my own life lessons through my own hard experiences and through my own pain. Likewise, you'll have to live through yours. I've received answers and understandings that I've had to work out, and I've spent a lot of time with God doing so. You'll need to do this too.

I can recommend a few places where you can find help. A good place to start is Viktor Frankl's book, *Man's Search for Meaning*. Viktor Frankl was a therapist and a Jew; he practiced around the time of the Nazis and World War II. Viktor spent much of that war in concentration camps.

In his book, which he wrote in just nine days after he was released, he described his experiences, but his more important goal was to address and answer the question: what is the purpose of suffering?

I also recommend the Bible. If you haven't already, take a look at that book. There's some good stuff in there, specifically the first three chapters of Job, and Job chapter 38 to the end.

I also recommend the four Gospels (Matthew, Mark, Luke, and John).

Take a look at Jesus's understanding of His purpose, and His calling, and the suffering that went with it.

(Yes, I know... I'm sounding quite cheery.)

It gets worse.

Not only do I believe that you cannot have vocational passion without suffering—and without understanding the purpose of suffering—I also believe that you cannot have vocational passion without working through my second point, which is:

Be faithful with the ordinary.

I can give you another personal perspective.

It seems to me that God will curb your pride, your selfishness, and the desire for recognition in order to build faithfulness, strength, and endurance by insisting that you deal with the ordinary.

At the Children's Home in Lubbock, day after day, I took care of the very basic needs of kids—all the time. From dressing, to bathing, to teaching how to go to the bathroom, to dealing with going to the bathroom, to going to the bathroom (there's a theme here), to cleaning up vomit... and on and on it went.

Even now, in my work as a crisis counselor with the police department, I deal with seemingly ordinary and mundane tasks—like, being called out at 3:00 a.m. to talk with a woman because her husband of 50 years has just died and because she has no other family... or sitting with some children whose parents are being arrested for drug possession... and doing that kind of thing over and over again in the wee hours of the morning, and without anyone else knowing.

God has been very patient (and relentless), but after several years of practice, I am finally coming to terms with dealing with the ordinary... peacefully and joyfully.

There is a principle you will find at work in God's Kingdom. And that principle is illustrated in a few of Jesus's parables, like the parable of the talents found in Matthew chapter 25.

When God gives you a little, He will then watch to see how faithful you are with it and what you are going to do with it. He waits to see if you will use it responsibly, or if you will waste it, and then decides if you can be trusted with more. If He finds you faithful and loving with just a little, He will create the opportunities for you to receive more. Your faithfulness with the ordinary may develop into a passion in various ways, even while you are still working in and with the ordinary. The phrase that comes to mind is "daily tasks performed in love." And the words that especially jump out at me are the words "in love."

There are many people sitting here today dealing with ordinary daily tasks. I don't think that being a student could be described any better than having to deal with and do ordinary, daily tasks. Actually, at some point in everyone's life, most any job deals with the ordinary and mundane.

The key here is: how do I do this task *in love*?

My third point about finding your vocational passion is short and to the point. It comes from 2 Corinthians 5:20 which says, "Therefore, we are ambassadors for Christ, as though God were entreating through us." (NASB 1977)

You are the Lord's ambassador, a representative of the Kingdom of Heaven, no matter where you are or what you are doing. I likewise consider myself an ambassador of the Almighty God, be it helping an abused child learn to use a bathroom, or standing in a stranger's living room, silently praying because their child has just died.

The fourth matter builds on the three previous thoughts. As you attempt to become passionate about your vocation or your calling, you may decide that it's utterly impossible. You simply don't like what you do. If this is the case, *you'll need to come to terms with God's sovereignty*.

Even as you continue to experience suffering in various ways, struggle with the ordinary, and strive your best to represent the Lord, you can find encouragement and even passion from the truth that *you have been called by the God of the universe into a vocation such as this*. Meanwhile, you'll find yourself in good company. I'm specifically referring to the Old Testament where you'll read about a few old prophets and other characters who, likewise, didn't really dig the hand that God dealt them.

Even though suffering, dealing with the ordinary, and acting as an ambassador may not be fun, these three experiences will actually help you to accept His calling and His sovereignty. Coming to terms with God's supreme power and authority, understanding that God knows you, and realizing that He has orchestrated your beginning so that it will relate to your end, will (in my view), open up all you need in order to thrive and have a passion for your vocation.

I've earned a degree in Bible, a master's in Youth and Family Ministry, and another in Community Counseling. So, of course, I'm now a professor in psychology and a crisis counselor with the police department. My path has made perfect sense.

This brings me to my fifth and last point.

We are to be *willing vessels, available, with a peaceful and open attitude.*

This is another part of finding your vocational passion.

I've worked more than 600 crisis calls with the police department—several homicides, probably 100 completed suicides, many child deaths, about 30 deceased infant calls, sexual assaults, domestic violence, officer deaths…and on and on it goes. And I've often been asked the question, "How have you been able to do that work for so long?" Another version of that question is, "Do you still like your job?" And it's usually asked in a tone like, "You're dumb."

So, I'll answer that question with a story from my life and my vocation.

I received a call from the police department to report to the hospital. An 11-year-old boy had been accidentally shot, and he was in surgery. An LCU student accompanied me, learning to do what I do; and when we walked into the ER, we met up with a police officer along with a rookie who was learning to do what she does. In one of the waiting rooms, about 30 family members and friends had shown up in the midst of this crisis.

I began to scan the crowd for the mother. But before I could find her, two very angry men came in and really started to make a mess. The police officer soon handed her camera to the rookie officer, got in those men's faces, and kindly asked them to depart. And they did.

Then, I again went about trying to find the mother of this child. About the time I figured out who she was, the surgeon came in and sat down to give her an update. The essence of what that surgeon said was, "This is not going well." Then the surgeon left.

And I saw the mom kind of relax. It looked as though she was a little relieved—which didn't make sense to me. The woman who was with the mother looked up at me with kind of a quizzical look, like, *Uh, something is wrong here.*

It was then apparent to both of us that the mom didn't hear the surgeon the way we did.

Hence, it seemed that part of my calling in that moment was to explain to the mom what I thought the surgeon said, and the essence was, "This is not going well."

She then looked up at me and said, "So…they are giving me time to prepare?"

I said, "Yes, ma'am. I think you need to prepare for the worst."

At that moment, reality started to sink in.

Eventually, a nurse came into the room and asked the entire crowd to move up to the pediatric ICU. So, we all went up there, and about 40 people were standing around.

Then the nurse came out once again and asked the mom to come back to the family room. She started to head that way when, all of a sudden, she stopped, turned around, and looked at me. Then she asked, "Will you come with me?" and I said, "Sure, I'll come with you."

At this point, I still didn't know her name. She and I then went back to the family room and sat down. After a few moments, a different doctor came in, sat down, and said what I knew was coming.

Looking at the mother, he said, "Your son has died."

And she fell to pieces.

I sat there quietly and prayed.

Immediately, the surgeon started to explain what would happen next. But she was just beginning to grieve, and understandably, couldn't quite deal with having to make decisions.

The doctor then became a bit frustrated. He looked at me with a look that said, "I'm frustrated."

And I looked at him, like, "You're dumb."

Finally, he gave up, kind of huffed, and left the room.

So, now, it was me and this woman, whom I had just met, sitting in this room.

This mother was getting her mind around what had just happened, and in the meantime, I sat there and allowed her to cry. My job was to simply be there for her.

Eventually, she stopped crying, and she was ready. We got up and went out to the waiting room. She gave the crowd the news. The grief reaction, the sound that came up from that crowd—well, I will never forget it. At some point later, a nurse came out and asked the mom, "Do you want to go see your son?"

I could see that she hadn't thought of that possibility. She quickly turned, looked at her friend, and her friend said, "Uh, I'm not sure what you should do."

Then the mom looked at me for my opinion.

"Ma'am," I said, "I usually tell people that you want to remember your loved one as they were and not how they might look at this moment. But, everybody is different."

She took a minute to think about what I said and then shook her head and said, "Nooo." Then she added, "I want to see him."

Naturally, I said, "All right."

I went back to the pediatric ICU, found a nurse, and then took a look at her son's body to get a feel for what she was about to see. Then I went back out and said, "Well, all right. Your son is in there, and he's got a drape up to here [sliding my hand across my chest]. And he's still got a tube in his mouth from when they were helping him to breathe. You don't want to move that drape because, you know, he just came out of surgery. That's basically what you'll see, so you'll need to ready yourself for this."

She said, "All right. I need to do this."

I said, "All right. I'll go with you."

Why Am I Still Doing This?

So, we walked down that long hall and into that room, this tall, skinny white guy and this little African-American woman.

We found that the nurses had set up a chair at the young boy's head, and when we walked past one of the nurses, she was doing like this [wiping the tears from her face].

Mom sat down next to her little boy, and for the next several minutes, she said good-bye.

Meanwhile, I stood next to her and prayed.

At one point, she looked up at me and she said, "You know that saying, 'All things happen for good'?"

She was quoting Romans 8:28[29], and she continued, "I don't believe that. I don't think it's true."

Nodding, I said, "Yes, ma'am. I totally understand that."

There was a pause. Then I added, "Ma'am, I believe that God is very close to those who are suffering, and I believe that He is very close to you right now."

She looked up at me, and she likewise nodded knowingly.

I was kind of surprised. I thought she might be irritated, even angry, with a glare that said, "How dare you say that to me!"

Instead, she simply nodded without any resentment.

That incident occurred in 2001. And as you can tell, that moment is still with me.

I didn't ask for my calling, but I am grateful for it. I wouldn't change anything about it.

When she was finished, that mother and I walked back out to the waiting room. And those two angry men from before—well, they showed up again, and they had the same attitude.

For whatever reason, I instinctively stepped in front of this woman as one of those men came cussing at her and blaming her for what had happened. It was dumb on my part. That's a cop's job. That's not my job.

---

[29] "And we know that all things work together for good to those who love God, to those who are the called according to His purpose" (Romans 8:28 New King James Version).

Anyway…when I stepped in between them, he continued to yell at her around me. In the next instant, an officer came from around the corner and scooped him up and convinced him to leave in a way that was pleasing to me.

Eventually, everything kind of settled down, and it was time for everybody to go home.

I walked with the mother out to the front of the hospital, and it was at that point that I said, "Ma'am, would you like me to give you a call in the morning or sometime tomorrow and see how you and your family are doing?"

And she said, "Yes, please."

I then asked, "Can you tell me your name?"

At that point, I learned her name, other pertinent information, and gave her a call the next day. And that ended my journey with her.

I think this story illustrates, as best I can, my view of finding your vocational passion.

In summary, my five points today are…

First: suffering is a part and a cost associated with finding your vocational passion. Understanding the true meaning of suffering and accepting it is key.

Second: being faithful (and even joyful) with the ordinary is also part of the deal.

Third: remember, you are the Lord's ambassador wherever He stations you, and you are always His ambassador.

Fourth: if you don't like your current vocation or calling, you'll need to come to terms with God's sovereignty.

Fifth: determine to become a willing, open, submitted, and peaceful vessel.

As you square away these five truths and settle them in your heart, I believe you'll find the freedom to passionately walk in your calling and your vocation as intended.

REFERENCES AND RESOURCES

For assistance with the grief associated with the death of a child, see www.compassionatefriends.org.

Frankl, V. (1959). *Man's Search for Meaning.* Boston, MA: Beacon Press.

Gilmartin, K. (2002). *Emotional Survival for Law Enforcement: A Guide for Officers and Their Families.* Tucson, AZ: E-S Press.

James, R., and Gilliland, B. (2013). *Crisis Intervention Strategies*, Boston, MA: Brooks/Cole Publishing.

Jamison, K. (2000). *Night Falls Fast: Understanding Suicide.* New York: Knopf Doubleday Publishing Group.

Kirshman, E. (2006). *I Love a Cop.* New York: Guilford Press.

Lord, J., and Stewart A. (2008). *I'll Never Forget Those Words: A Practical Guide to Death Notification.* Compassion Press.

Mitchell, J., and Everly, G. (2001). *Critical Incident Stress Debriefing: An Operations Manual for CISD, Defusing and Other Group Crisis Intervention Services.* Columbia, MD: Chevron Publishing.

Pinizzotto, A., Kern, H., and Davis, E. (2004). *One-Shot Drops: Surviving the Myth*. FBI Law Enforcement Bulletin. Federal Bureau of Investigation, U.S. Department of Justice, October.

Young, A., Fuller, J., and Riley, B. (2008). *On-scene Mental Health Counseling Provided Through Police Departments*. Journal of Mental Health Counseling. Volume 30, Number 4. 345-361.

Young, A., and Brumley, N. (September, 2009). *On-scene Mental Health Services: A Case Study of the Lubbock Police Department's Victims Services Crisis Team*. FBI Law Enforcement Bulletin. 6-11.

ABBREVIATIONS

EMS – Emergency Medical Services

LPC – Licensed Professional Counselor

ME – Medical Examiner

MH – Mental Health

SWAT – Special Weapons and Tactics

TPI – Third-Party Intermediary

GLOSSARY

Bad guy – Someone who obviously committed a crime and is probably the focus of the attention of law enforcement.

Break-and-rake – A SWAT maneuver in which a group of officers approaches a window; and while some officers are covering that window with their weapons, another uses a tool to break the window and rake out the glass and other obstructions.

Cognitive reaction – Reacting to a stressful situation from a rational, and usually calm internal place. Thinking things through, looking at logical consequences, and remaining relatively objective.

Command post – In the case of a SWAT callout, it is the area in which commanders and chiefs have gathered to command and control the crisis response. Often the command post begins as command staff gathered in the street together, and then moves to a mobile command post like a departmental RV that is outfitted for such an event.

Counsel – To give someone truth to consider.

Counseling/counselor – In the state of Texas it is someone who has obtained a graduate degree in counseling or related field, taken the state licensing exam, completed three thousand hours of supervised counseling, and now operates according to the standards of practice outlined by the state board of ethics.

Crisis – An event that overwhelms an individual's ability to cope.

Crisis intervention or Psychological first aid – Methods and strategies for assisting people in crisis and the situations surrounding a crisis.

Critical Incident Stress Management (CISM) – A model and protocols by Mitchell and Everly designed to assist emergency services personnel with psychologically processing stressful or traumatic events.

Death notification – The process of informing a person about the death of a loved one.

Debriefing – A meeting that gives a group of emergency services personnel a chance to psychologically and emotionally process a traumatic experience. Typically, this meeting is comprised of a homogeneous group of people (e.g., all police officers) who were equally exposed to the traumatic event.

Defusing – A short meeting for a homogeneous group of emergency services personnel, giving participants the opportunity to discuss a traumatic event in order to assist them to psychologically process and cope.

Demobilization – A short meeting conducted to disperse information regarding coping mechanisms in order to help emergency services personnel make the transition from a traumatic event at work to heading home.

Glossary

Diagnostic and Statistical Manual of Mental Disorders - V – The current edition of the Manual that contains information, including the diagnostic criteria, about psychological disorders.

Domestic violence – Violence perpetrated by a family member upon another family member.

Emergency medical services (EMS) – A service that provides emergency medical care outside of the hospital. Emergency medical technicians and paramedics typically provide this care.

Emergency rescue vehicle (ERV) and The Bear – These are armored personnel carriers used by the police department in situations where the risk of gunfire is present.

Emotional reaction – Typically a reaction to a circumstance demonstrated by emotions such as anger, sadness, and fear.

Explosive ordinance disposal (EOD) – A unit within a police department or military entity trained and responsible for the safe handling and disposal of explosive devices.

Gallows humor – A type of humor that is found in dark and depressing situations, usually used as a coping mechanism. I have many examples, but I fear they all could be offensive, especially without proper attitude and context.

Good guy – Everyone who is not a bad guy.

Homicide – When a person's death is caused by the actions of another person.

Hostage – Someone held by force against their will.

Medical examiner – A physician licensed by the state to investigate the medical causes of a death.

Mental health professional – A general term from someone educated and usually licensed by the state as a counselor, social worker, therapist, psychologist, psychiatrist, etc.

Natural death – Death by natural cause, such as disease.

Hostage or crisis negotiator – A specially-trained law enforcement officer who often responds to SWAT callouts and other situations where dialogue with someone may assist in the peaceful resolution of an incident.

> Primary negotiator – A negotiator who speaks directly to a subject.
>
> Secondary negotiator – A negotiator who assists the primary negotiator and serves as the funnel through which all communication with the primary negotiator passes.

Neighborhood services – A division within the police department that focuses on interaction and liaison with the community.

Police titles in order of rank:

> Cadet – A person training to be a police officer through a police academy.
>
> Patrolman - A police officer of entry rank assigned to the patrol division of a department.
>
> Deputy – A law enforcement officer in a County Sheriff's Department.
>
> Corporal – A rank above that of police officer.

Glossary

Sergeant – A police officer of middle rank, below that of lieutenant, usually responsible for the supervision of officers and corporals.

Lieutenant – A police officer that ranks above that of sergeant and usually denotes command responsibilities.

Captain – A police officer of high rank, above that of lieutenant, that typically is responsible for command decisions.

Assistant Chief – A commander in charge of a large division within a police department (e.g. Patrol or Investigations).

Chief of police – The most senior police officer in charge of all police within a city or jurisdiction.

Commissioner – A police officer in charge of a particular police force.

Sheriff – The most senior law enforcement officer in a county.

Cop – A term for police officer that is usually not derogative.

Detective – A police officer that investigates criminal activity and presents findings to a district attorney.

State trooper – A police officer who is a member of a state police force.

Post-traumatic stress disorder (PTSD) – A psychological disorder that is caused by exposure to a traumatic event and includes specific symptoms from a list of categories such as avoidance (i.e., avoiding things associated with the traumatic event), intrusion (e.g., nightmares), and hypervigilance (i.e., being jumpy or on guard).

Psychopath – Also referred to as a sociopath and sometimes as someone who has Antisocial Personality Disorder (APD). I prefer the view that a psychopath is a violent and criminal version of APD. APD is characterized by lack of empathy and intimacy, by manipulativeness, deceitfulness, callousness, hostility, irresponsibility, and impulsivity. In general, this person is egocentric in their drive for personal gain, likes being in control, having power, lives for personal gratification, and does not conform to society's norms.

Suicide – Purposefully causing one's own death.

Suicide by cop – Putting a law enforcement officer in the position of having to use deadly force for the purpose of causing one's own death.

SWAT (Special Weapons and Tactics) callout – A law enforcement incident that requires a specialized response by officers specially trained and outfitted with the proper equipment. SWAT callouts typically involve responding to heavily-armed subjects, barricaded subjects, hostage situations, and other incidents not easily or safely handled by patrol officers.

Third-party intermediary (TPI) – Using someone as a go-between during the process of negotiations.

Victim Services Crisis Team (VSCT) – A group of mental health professionals whose response is initiated by law enforcement in order to assist officers and/or civilians with a crisis situation.

Glossary

Mental Health Professionals learning to drive police cars.

FIGHT OR FLIGHT

The three coolest Crisis Team volunteers.

VICTIM SERVICES CRISIS TEAM

LUBBOCK POLICE DEPARTMENT

ABOUT THE AUTHOR

Andy Young received a bachelor's degree in Bible from Lubbock Christian University in 1993, a master's degree in Youth and Family Ministry from Abilene Christian University in 1995, a master's in Community Counseling from Texas Tech University in 1999, and a doctorate in Counselor Education from Texas Tech University in 2003. He has been a professor at Lubbock Christian University since 1996 and currently teaches in the undergraduate Behavioral Sciences Department and graduate Nursing Department. He has also taught in the graduate Counseling and undergraduate Bible Departments.

Working with the Lubbock Police Department since 2000 and the Lubbock County Sheriff's Office since 2008, Andy also currently serves on the negotiating teams for both agencies. Additionally, he acts as clinical director for the Critical Incident Stress Management Teams for the South Plains Regional Response Team, the Lubbock Police Department, and the Lubbock Fire Department.

Young is also a founding member and current coordinator for the Lubbock Police Department's Victim Services Crisis Team, which has grown to about 40 members. He is the author of several published academic articles and speaks frequently on crisis intervention and hostage negotiation, most recently at hostage negotiator conferences sponsored by various state associations including California, Washington, and Texas.

Andy and his wife, Stacy, who were married in 1995, live in Lubbock, Texas with their two children.

CONTACT DR. ANDY YOUNG

www.drandyyoung.com

www.fightorflightbook.com

andy.young@lcu.edu

Generation Culture Transformation
Specializing in publishing for generation culture change

Visit us Online at:
www.egen.co

Write to: eGenCo
824 Tallow Hill Road
Chambersburg, PA 17202 USA
Phone: 717-461-3436
Email: info@egen.co

facebook.com/egenbooks

youtube.com/egenpub

egen.co/blog

pinterest.com/eGenDMP

twitter.com/eGenDMP

instagram.com/egenco_dmp

Made in the USA
Lexington, KY
25 June 2016